Shade Gardens

Shade Gardens

by
OLIVER E. ALLEN
and
the Editors of TIME-LIFE BOOKS

TIME-LIFE BOOKS, ALEXANDRIA, VIRGINIA

THE TIME-LIFE ENCYCLOPEDIA OF GARDENING

THE AUTHOR: Oliver E. Allen is a former staff member of LIFE magazine and of TIME-LIFE BOOKS, where he served as Editor of the LIFE World Library and the TIME-LIFE Library of America. He also wrote Decorating With Plants and Pruning and Grafting for The TIME-LIFE Encyclopedia of Gardening.

CONSULTANTS: James Underwood Crockett, author of 13 of the volumes in the Encyclopedia, co-author of two additional volumes and consultant on other books in the series, has been a lover of the earth and its good things since his boyhood on a Massachusetts fruit farm. He was graduated from the Stockbridge School of Agriculture at the University of Massachusetts and has worked ever since in horticulture. A perennial contributor to leading gardening magazines, he also writes a monthly bulletin, "Flowery Talks," that is widely distributed through retail florists. His television program, Crockett's Victory Garden, shown all over the United States, has won millions of converts to the Crockett approach to growing things. Els Benjamin, horticulturist, is Acting Director at Brookside Gardens, Wheaton, Md. Dr. T. R. Dudley is Research Botanist at the U.S. National Arboretum in Washington, D.C. Harold Epstein is editor of the Brooklyn Botanic Garden Handbook Gardening in the Shade and President Emeritus of the American Rock Garden Society. Dr. Henry T. Skinner is former Director of the National Arboretum in Washington, D.C., and Vice President of the Royal Horticultural Society at Wisley, England. Dr. William Louis Stern is Professor of Botany at the University of Maryland, College Park.

THE COVER: Once host to nothing but weeds, the shaded area beneath the spreading boughs of a Douglas fir in Tacoma, Washington, has been transformed into a thriving circular bed of ferns, shrubs, bulbs and other ground covers. In the foreground, the white-rimmed foliage of silveredge goutweed surrounds the fronds of a parsley fern and intermingles with the dainty flowers of yellow corydalis (right). Nearer the center of the bed are several azaleas and rhododendrons—all of them pruned low to accentuate the curving limbs of the tree.

Library of Congress Cataloging in Publication Data
Allen, Oliver E.
    Shade gardens
    (The Time-Life encyclopedia of gardening)
    Bibliography: p.
    Includes index.
    1. Gardening in the shade. I. Time-Life Books.
II. Title.
SB434.7.A44   635.9'54   79-10953
ISBN 0-8094-2647-1
ISBN 0-8094-2646-3 lib. bdg.

CONTENTS

The shady side of gardening 1

On a steep, rocky suburban hillside near New York City, just a quarter of a mile from a bustling suburban center and only a hundred yards from a busy parkway, there is a garden that completely blocks out the encroaching urban world. Winding pathways of pine needles and wood chips, informal steps and landings, and pleasant seating areas beckon the visitor into an idealized woodland. Luxurious expanses of pachysandra, periwinkle, ivy and ajuga carpet the ground. Above them rise ferns, azaleas, rhododendrons, dogwoods, yews, small hemlocks and hollies. Surmounting these are the high branches of beeches, tulip trees, a hickory and an old oak.

From early June to midautumn, few rays of direct sunlight touch this garden, nor are they missed. The green shadows are cool and restful on a hot day, serene and reassuring. It is, says its owner, "a place to go when you feel bothered and want to get away." At the same time, it is anything but dull. Everyone who enters it is astonished and intrigued by the richness and variety of its plant life. How does it happen that shade, reputed to be so hostile to growing things, could yield such a flourishing retreat?

The answer is that many people make wrong assumptions about shade. Every time the shadow of a tree or a building falls across their domain, they think it spells disaster to their plantings. What these gardeners do not realize is that many plants not only grow in shade but actually prefer it—and that an even greater number perform well under either condition, since their need is not for the sun but for a certain level of light intensity. This gives the gardener with shade a choice of plants to suit virtually every imaginable circumstance.

The garden mentioned above, for example, is almost solidly green in midsummer. But it need not be. A few score miles away, in a garden shaded by stately tulip trees, the owners maintain a constantly unfolding succession of bloom under their leafy canopy.

Nestled in the shade of an old oak tree, hostas brighten a quiet sylvan garden. The lush foliage of these hardy perennials thrives even in deep shade, but more light is needed to bring plants into bloom.

In midsummer, long after the daffodils, trilliums and azaleas have finished their spectacular spring show, the deep green of the rhododendron leaves is brightened by puffy balls of pale blue hydrangea blooms and the yellow flags of day lilies. Brilliant red cardinal flowers enliven a corner where a gray-green Japanese painted fern and the lacy white flower spires of bugbane also grow. And here and there can be seen yellow blooms on clumps of corydalis.

The expertise and imagination of these gardeners would stand many another homeowner in good stead, for shade is a conspicuous feature of a growing number of American gardens. People who bought houses twenty years ago, then prudently set out head-high saplings, now find themselves with sizable shade trees. In older communities existing trees cast ever-increasing shade; in cities the shadows of tall buildings fall across the gardens of row houses and the balconies and terraces of apartments. One nurseryman observes that his best-selling plant used to be the sun-loving petunia. Now, he says, everyone wants impatiens, a plant that thrives in shade.

A DELICATE ARRANGEMENT

Not only is shade prevalent, it is for many gardeners desirable. Shade gardens are subtle and enticing. Colors and textures are finely differentiated, and the observer is keenly aware of such qualities as form and scale. Instead of working with big gobs of color, the gardener finds himself composing textured arrangements of perennials and shrubs, rocks, grasses, sometimes even mosses, and using the natural configurations of such things as bark and tree roots as part of his design. When he does introduce flowering plants, he is likely to do so cautiously because flowers that bloom in the shade often have intense, demanding colors and are slow to fade.

One expert on shade gardens argues that in most regions of the United States and Canada shade plants are easier to grow than those that need sun. "They suffer less insect damage and require less attention," he says. "If you live in a temperate zone in what was once a woodland environment, the plants that will do best for you are those that are at home in the shade."

But what exactly is shade? There are many kinds and degrees, and everyone with a shaded garden should be able to distinguish among them. Many plants, for example, are described as growing well "under trees"—but different trees, even deciduous ones, cast different kinds of shadows. There is the relatively deep shade of beeches and Norway maples and the lighter shade of trees with sparser foliage, such as honey locusts, willow oaks and sweet gums. Trees with high branches cast a softer shade than those that branch near the ground. The shade of narrow trees like Lombardy poplars is inconstant, changing by the hour, while anything growing directly

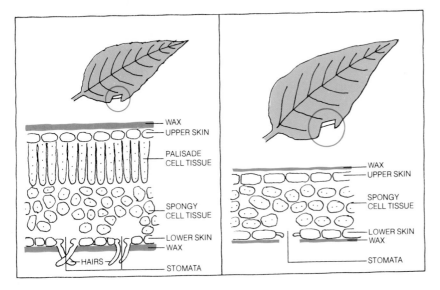

beneath a wide-spreading tree is likely to be in shadow most of the day. There is also a difference in the quality of shade. The dappled shade of a garden over which sunlight plays intermittently is not at all like the open shade on the north side of a house, where there is continuous skyshine but no direct sunlight.

SHADOWS CLASSIFIED

For purposes of definition and discussion, shade may be divided into three categories. The first is deep shade and it is the most restrictive of the three. Beneath low-branched pines or hemlocks the shade may be so dense that only a handful of plants have an outside chance of surviving in it—such tolerant woodland natives as wintergreen, Canada mayflower, ground pine or an occasional fern.

As deep shade becomes a bit less dense, however, the possibilities begin to open up. Deep but less Stygian shade—still in the first category—will be found near the base of the north side of a high wall, under lower-branching trees like dogwood, viburnum and redbud, and under the higher or more openly branching hemlocks or other evergreens. A considerable number of plants will survive in these conditions, including several ground covers like ivy, pachysandra, ajuga, violets and almost all ferns. Hostas will grow in such deep shade, but only as foliage plants; for bloom in deep shade you can move potted tropical house plants outdoors for the summer.

With higher branching and wider spacing of the overhead canopy, deep shade fades into medium shade, the second category. This is the kind you like to sit in on a hot summer day: there is plenty of light around you but very little direct sun. It is found under higher-branching or more sparsely foliaged deciduous trees, in areas shaded by north-facing walls but otherwise unobstructed, or in areas illuminated by reflected sunlight. Medium shade provides enough light to bring into bloom flowering plants like wax begonias, impatiens and day lilies as well as flowering shrubs like oak-leaved hydrangea and rosebay rhododendron. In fact, almost any plant will survive in medium shade, although it will not necessarily prosper—you could grow roses there but they probably would not bloom.

SOMETIMES, THE SUN

In the final category, open or intermittent shade, the shade of high-branched trees that are even more widely spaced, the garden receives direct sunlight in varying degrees adding up to three or four hours a day—perhaps in the morning, at midday or in the afternoon. By seizing these fleeting rays, the shade gardener can even take a chance with some sun-loving plants. They will not bloom as prodigiously as they do in full sun, but they may bloom nonetheless.

Intermittent shade includes the dappled light of sun that shines between leaves, the shifting filtered light beneath arbors and trellises, and the light that strikes gardens only seasonally. Many gardens become shady, for instance, only after trees leaf out. In such gardens you can take advantage of the spring sun to grow daffodils and many other early-flowering bulbs, spring-blooming wildflowers and such early perennials as primroses and forget-me-nots. There are also gardens that may be alternately sunny or shady at certain other times of the year, depending on the angle of the sun.

THE ROLE OF CLIMATE

Complicating the selection of plants for these various conditions of shade is climate. For some plants, temperature is as important as light, and they respond accordingly. In cool regions they flourish in sunlight; in warm regions they prefer shade. Roses, for example, do best in full sunlight in northern states, but in Florida they benefit

SETTLING FOR LESS LIGHT

During the course of a day, plants are exposed to many different intensities of light, depending on the angle of the sun's rays and on the thickness of the atmosphere through which the rays pass. At sunrise, those rays travel farther to reach the plant than they do at midday, and their intensity may be further diffused by mists. Thus, from zero foot-candles half an hour before dawn, light intensity may climb to 10,000 foot-candles at high noon on a cloudless June 21 in Washington, D.C. For shade plants, the light intensity required may be one tenth the maximum amount produced by the midday sun, and even sun-loving plants need only one quarter to one third of this amount.

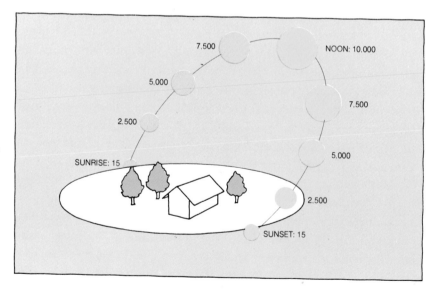

from the protection of intermediate shade. Furthermore, few shade plants native to the West Coast will thrive in East Coast shade gardens, even when the soil structure is corrected to correspond to that of their origins. However, Japanese shade plants do very well in the eastern United States. Given these variants in plant behavior, it is wise to check your choices with a knowledgeable shade gardener in your neighborhood and with a local nurseryman.

While the growing conditions of gardening in the shade are restrictive, they can frequently be modified. Shade, if it is caused by several trees, can be lightened by removing a tree or two. As a less drastic measure, their branches can be pruned to allow more light to pass through. You can do this either by thinning the principal branches so the tree has less foliage, or by removing lower branches, raising the shade canopy farther from the ground. One experienced shade gardener keeps all his tall oaks clear of branches to a point 50 feet in the air, letting in more light not only from above but also from the sides. For safety's sake this is a job for tree surgeons. "But," he says, "I don't regret a penny I've spent on it. The quality of the light below is immensely improved."

One important by-product of pruning is that it also improves air circulation. When trees and plants are too thick, they impede the flow of air essential to their health. This is especially true of shade plants, which do not have sunlight to help keep their foliage dry. In fact, it is a good idea to thin not only the canopy trees but the smaller trees beneath them. Even the shade-growing shrubs can benefit from judicious pruning: plants that grow in low illumination tend to become leggy in their upward journey toward the light.

OPENING THE CANOPY

SOME LIKE IT COOL

For many plants, too much sunlight can be as critical as too little. When the light intensity rises, so does the temperature—and heat can affect a plant's well-being even more than illumination. Temperature, in fact, is a main reason that sun-loving plants in cool regions become shade plants in hot climates. In selecting a shaded area for plants that prefer coolness, note that the temperature beneath most deciduous trees is likely to be higher than that beneath ground-hugging evergreens, and temperatures are generally lower at ground level than several feet above. Also, a hillside is usually warmer than a swale because cold air (arrows) will flow into a depression and collect there.

The roots of the problem

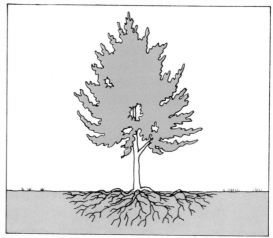

The trees that cloak your garden in shade can contribute to the health of smaller plants by showering them with a mineral-rich mulch of leaves, but some trees also rob these plants of necessary nutrients and moisture. It all depends on the nature of their root systems. Deep-rooted trees such as oaks are noncompetitive, but shallow-rooted trees like maples draw much of their sustenance from the same soil level as the smaller plants, leaving the soil so dry or impoverished that only mosses will grow under the trees.

Sometimes aggressive tree roots can be blocked by an underground barrier (*page 14*) if their habit of growth is horizontal. But barriers do little good in blocking insidious roots like those of the tulip tree, which simply duck under any obstruction and come up on the other side. With certain trees, however, like maples, it is possible to remove a single large root and all its feeder roots close to the surface of the soil (*below*), temporarily creating a narrow root-free planting bed without doing serious damage to the tree.

PREPARING A ROOT-FREE BED

To create a planting bed under a tree with a shallow, many-branched root system, expose a root near the trunk and cut it off clean, using an ax or a hatchet. Remove the severed root from the soil, using a spade and the hatchet again, if necessary, to dislodge it. Cultivate the newly made garden bed to about two spade depths, using fresh topsoil or the old soil enriched with soil conditioners.

Just as a lack of air circulation may hinder the growth of plants aboveground, so does congestion beneath the soil. Often the problems of gardening beneath trees result not from the shade itself but from other conditions caused by the trees. Roots are among the chief villains. The shallow root systems of those old American favorites, the maple, beech and elm, are the bane of shade gardeners. Not only do they make digging difficult, but they suck up moisture and nutrients, leaving very little for less aggressive plants.

Short of replacing shallow-rooted trees with deep-rooted ones, there is not much that can be done about this situation. If you add a heavy extra layer of soil to what is already there, either you may kill the tree or the new soil will be filled with tree roots in one season. If you thin out some of the small feeder roots, chances are they will grow back before your plants become established unless the thinning has been drastic. The best course is to plant a ground cover that needs relatively little moisture and nourishment, such as one of the trailing sedums or ivy. Or you can give up trying to plant the root area and cover it with river gravel or flagstones.

If there is not much you can do to alter a shallow root system, you can change some of the other elements in the picture. The most important of these is soil. Often the soil in shady areas is excessively acid hard-packed clay. If moss is growing here and there, the soil probably is poorly drained, very acid and lacking in fertility.

SOIL CONDITIONING

To improve the soil it is necessary to loosen it and adjust its components. As you do, keep in mind the seemingly contradictory nature of good soil: it must drain well in moist periods and retain water during dry spells. Little more than half the bulk of most soils is made up of solid matter; the rest is air, little gaps between the grains of soil like the gaps between rocks in a rock pile. When you water the soil, these spaces fill up. Ideally the water will quickly drain away, leaving just a film of moisture held by each solid particle. The roots of your plants thus have access to both oxygen and water.

In clay soils these air spaces are tiny and drain slowly; in sandy soils, there are fewer spaces, but they are large and drain quickly. Both types are likely to be short on humus, the decayed animal or vegetable matter that provides nourishment and water-holding capacity. Your aim is to correct all three problems and end up with soil that is about half clay, one fourth sand, and at least one fourth organic material. Such a soil has what gardeners call good tilth—it is loose and easily worked but not excessively so.

INS AND OUTS OF WATER

To attack problem soil, first examine its physical composition. Dig a hole about a foot deep when the soil is dry and feel the texture of the soil at that level. If it is fine-textured but extremely stiff, almost like hard plaster, it is basically clay. If it is gritty and falls apart whether wet or dry, it is basically sand. If it is light in color, it is almost certainly lacking in humus, for decayed organic material is always dark. Now fill the hole with water. If it does not drain away in a hour or so, your soil is all but impenetrable.

Unless you plan to have a bog garden, which needs a damp, stagnant soil, your top priority is to correct a soil that remains wet for too long a time after a rain by providing some means for excess water to drain away. One solution is to install underground perforated plastic drainage pipes over a layer of gravel to carry water to a lower level. This may be necessary if the soil is extremely soggy, but it is also difficult. Another solution, which will yield a similar result, is to dig out a planting bed to a depth of two feet and cover the bottom of the excavation with a six-inch layer of coarse builder's sand, providing a drainage outlet from the sand layer by digging a trench, putting in a layer of gravel, then filling the trench. Refill the planting area with a proper soil mix.

A GYPSUM TREATMENT

If your investigations have shown that the soil has too much clay, loosen it by mixing in coarse builder's sand. You can also use gypsum—calcium sulfate—to make clay soil more friable; it is available at many garden centers. In time the calcium ions in the gypsum will replace the blotter-like sodium ions naturally present in

BARRIERS AGAINST ROOTS AND RAIN

A 2½-foot-wide collar of rigid plastic will prevent shallow-rooted bamboo from invading nearby areas. Bury the collar with its upper edge at soil level. A bottomless galvanized tub will serve the same purpose.

Annuals or perennials requiring acid soil can be planted in the shadow of a masonry wall if their roots are shielded from the lime that is leached out of the wall. Dig a trench 2 inches wide and 9 inches deep next to the

wall. Place a 9-inch-wide strip of rigid plastic against the outer side of the trench and fill it with gravel or sand (inset). Rain hitting the wall will sink into the trench instead of soaking into the soil around the plants.

the clay, leaving the clay crumbly and with good air spaces rather than tightly packed.

Now add humus. For greatest efficiency and lowest cost, the humus should come from your own compost pile. If you are just starting to garden and do not have a ready supply of compost, leaf mold, peat moss, dried manure or rotting hay can be used instead.

To improve sandy soil, you have several options. You can add quantities of peat moss, although you may be startled by the large amount needed. An alternative is to add clay. One shade gardener ordered a truckload of clay to improve the texture of his light, sandy soil; it confounded his friends but turned out to be just what was needed. Sand is only a soil conditioner, not an enricher, but clay contains most of the nutrients necessary for plant growth. Nevertheless, in either case you will still have to add organic material to retain moisture. Probably the simplest way to correct a sandy soil is to mix in good topsoil from a reputable nursery.

The final step in adjusting your soil is to check its chemical balance. Soils range from acid to alkaline on a pH scale of 1 to 14, with 7 being neutral, anything below 7 acid, and anything above 7 alkaline. For most plants you are likely to want to grow, a reading between 6 and 7 is excellent, but a few plants that are especially desirable for shade, like rhododendrons, azaleas and mountain laurels, prefer a more acid soil, between 4.5 and 6.5. The test itself can be done with a soil test kit obtainable at most garden centers. Or you can send samples of your soil to the local office of the Cooperative Extension Service to be tested.

Most soils in areas once forested tend to be slightly acid; alkaline soils are more common in areas of limited rainfall, as in the Far West, or in areas with limestone rock formations. The addition of humus to improve a soil's texture may reduce its acidity somewhat, but if it needs additional correcting, add ground limestone, about five pounds per 100 square feet to raise the pH one point. To make soil more acid add peat moss or leaf mold made from oak leaves, or, following package directions, dig in a mixture of equal parts of superphosphate, ammonium sulfate and powdered sulfur, a combination that may be found premixed at garden centers.

Once you have given your shade garden the best possible start with deep digging to remove surface tree roots, with the addition of leaf mold and any other needed ingredients, and with provision for air circulation and light, be prepared to encourage its development with regular feeding and watering. One of the biggest misconceptions about gardening in the shade is that the soil does not dry out because it is not in the sun. On the contrary, it requires just as much

THE CHEMICAL BALANCE

VITAL MOISTURE

MULCHING OVER BARREN SOIL

When the soil beneath a shallow-rooted tree proves unplantable, you can dress it up with a decorative mulch. Organic mulches like wood chips, bark or pine needles will enrich the soil as they decay but they need replacement more frequently. Organic mulches should be 2 to 3 inches deep, inorganic mulches like river gravel about half that depth. To keep them looking neat, install an edging of bricks, flagstones or preservative-treated garden timbers. Sink the edging flush with the lawns to facilitate mowing.

water as the sunny parts of the garden, and sometimes more. It is not uncommon to come upon sprinklers whirling in midsummer in well-tended shade gardens—even gardens that feel cool and damp. There is competition, particularly from the inevitable tree roots, for all the moisture that is available. Just how much water you add depends on your site, on its drainage and on the kind of plants you are growing. But when you water, be sure to water deeply, especially in hot weather and in late summer when leaf buds are forming and some shrubs are forming buds for the following season's flowers.

One way to help your shade garden retain moisture is to mulch it, and mulches perform other services too. A proper mulch can suppress weeds, moderate the effects of sudden fluctuations in temperature and prevent the carefully loosened soil from recompacting. If your mulch is an organic material, it will also contribute humus to the soil as it decomposes and will spur the work of soil microorganisms that help to nourish your plants. Mulch means mellow in the original German, *molsch,* and that is the characteristic that good mulches give to soil.

Organic mulches include such disparate materials as pine needles, crumbled leaves, buckwheat hulls, half-rotted compost, cottonseed and peanut hulls, seaweed, straw, wood chips, bark and even coffee grounds. Inorganic mulches include gravel, crushed stone and marble chips. Many low-growing ground covers also have a mulching effect. The choice of a mulch is partly one of taste. Some, like leaves, produce a naturalized effect, while others, like marble chips or buckwheat hulls, make the garden look more formal.

But choice is also dictated by practical concerns. If you use any sort of wood-based mulch, you may have to fertilize your garden more frequently, especially if the wood is freshly cut. Wood draws nitrogen-fixing bacteria from the soil in the process of decomposing, and nitrogen is essential to good foliage growth. A mulch of grass clippings may form a matted surface that repels water instead of allowing it to pass through unless the clippings are occasionally disturbed; finely ground peat moss is even more prone to this water-shedding shingle effect if it dries and cakes. Maple leaves, which compact as they decay, produce a similar problem. But oak leaves do not, because in decomposing they simply curl and crumble. Organic mulches need frequent replenishing since, to be effective, they should be two or more inches deep. Inorganic mulches can be much thinner, but they do nothing to replenish the soil's fertility.

Some shade gardeners practice a two-stage mulching system, changing their mulches semiannually. In the autumn they allow fallen leaves to remain on the ground to enrich the soil as they decompose. In the winter, the boughs of the Christmas tree and branches pruned from evergreens are added, partly to hold down the leaves. Then, in spring, the leaves are raked up and the ground is allowed to warm, to speed the emergence of spring-flowering wild-flowers and bulbs. When these fade, a summer mulch is applied. This, in turn, comes off in September to await more falling leaves. But less ambitious gardeners will be content to cultivate occasionally, to let leaves disintegrate on the ground and to apply additional spring or summer mulch only when the garden seems to need it.

A NUTRITIOUS DIET

Even though organic mulches take care of some of a garden's nourishment, you will want to enrich the soil further. One expert shade gardener pulls back the mulch around her perennials each spring, scratches into the soil a fertilizer high in phosphorus to encourage root development, and then replaces the mulch. A more economical though slower-acting method is to use compost, which also contains the nutrients plants need. A compost pile is a good place to put some of those leaves that have provided your garden with shade. Any other vegetable matter can also go into the pile, including kitchen scraps, tea leaves, coffee grounds and wood ashes (but not the ashes of charcoal briquets; they resist decay to the point that they have virtually no nutritive value). One suburbanite replenishes his compost pile by picking up bags full of grass clippings that his noncomposting neighbors have put out for the trash pickup.

Some keepers of compost piles are very scientific. They use special containers, or build special bins out of cinder blocks, and maintain several piles at once in various stages of decomposition. They arrange their material in layers, adding a thin blanket of soil occasionally, and they keep the entire pile moist. Their reward is excellent humus in about six months. But even gardeners who simply throw their compost in a heap eventually end up with equally excellent humus—although at a slower two- or three-year pace.

A garden that is well supplied with compost will encourage plants other than the cultivated ones for which the enrichment is intended. Weeds, even though they are held in check by mulch, may thrive in a woodland environment. But shade gardeners are more tolerant of them than other kinds of gardeners. Some gardeners, as they rout the more invasive species, occasionally allow interesting weeds to develop, just to see what they will produce. For one gardener this led to a serendipitous bonus, one of the delights of even a well-planned shade garden. After relentlessly pulling a weed that persisted in growing under an oak tree near his house, he gave up and let it grow. In September it produced a lovely nosegay of dainty white flowers and turned out to be a wild aster.

Shade plants for all seasons

"There ought to be gardens for all the months of the year, in which, severally, things of beauty may be then in season," declared 17th Century English essayist Sir Francis Bacon. Among his suggested plants for a year-round "princelike" garden were yew, violet, hyacinth, ivy, crocus, lily, holly, anemone and periwinkle—all excellent shade plants. Three centuries later these plants, together with many others that are shade tolerant, perform the same function in less princely surroundings, bringing year-round pleasure to home gardens canopied by trees or flanked by shade-casting walls.

To achieve a shade garden with seasonal shifts of mood can be remarkably simple, requiring only a few plants. In the wooded garden opposite, spring brings an awakening of color as a white azalea bursts into bloom and a Japanese maple unfurls its plum-colored leaves. Summer turns the garden into a soothing oasis of lush textured foliage. With autumn comes a rustling revival of color as the leaves of the maple turn burnt orange and a carpet of russet oak leaves covers the grass. Winter reveals a stark study in contrasts of barren branches, snow-encrusted bark and evergreen bamboo silhouetted against the white winter sky.

The most sought-after plants for a year-round shade garden are naturally those whose beauty endures and even heightens through more than one season. In addition to sprays of spring flowers, for example, the Korean rhododendron offers silver-green leaves that turn yellow or shades of red in the autumn. A vernal witch hazel produces fragrant ribbon-like flowers in late winter after a fall prelude of brilliant yellow foliage. And shade-tolerant evergreens like yew and hemlock are useful all year. In summer, they function as backdrops for the lighter foliage of deciduous plants; in winter, they move into the foreground to keep the garden visually alive.

Add some seasonal accent plants, such as hyacinths and crocuses, which bloom briefly and disappear beneath longer-lasting ground covers, and the year-round shade garden becomes more intriguing than a sun-drenched garden that dies at summer's end.

Under the shade of high-branching oaks, an azalea, a Japanese maple and a tall clump of evergreen bamboo create a composition that changes with the season.

Bursting into spring bloom

In spring, before trees overhead block the sun with their leaves, a shade garden comes alive with early-blooming bulbs, perennials, shrubs and flowering trees. From a 30-foot dogwood to a three-inch crocus, these plants can add a splash of spring color to almost any corner of a shady garden. Azaleas and rhododendrons will hug a steep bank. Trees that bloom before they leaf, such as redbuds, dogwoods or shadblows, will fill in high open spaces under the branches of an oak or ash tree. Primroses and marsh marigolds will carpet a rocky swale. Wild blue phlox will thrive in moist pockets among shallow maple roots. And many shade-tolerant perennials that bloom in spring, like epimediums, make fine edging plants because they are low growing and have attractive foliage.

Framed by a window for indoor viewing, a woodland garden explodes with spring flowers. The white ground cover is candytuft; behind it are pink rhododendrons and a lacy frieze of flowering dogwoods.

Yellow primroses, violet phlox and white snow trilliums bloom beneath an oak tree in the thin spring sun. To help these hardy woodland perennials retain moisture, they have been mulched with wood chips.

On an embankment in a wooded setting above his driveway, the owner of this shade garden gradually planted an amphitheater

of hundreds of azaleas, most grown from cuttings, and provided a bench so that spectators can sit and enjoy the spring show.

The serenity of summer

In a shade garden, summer is the season of richly contrasting textures and subtle colors. Foliage plants take center stage, while those with flowers slip quietly into the wings. Ferns play an important role because, with few exceptions, these lacy-leaved plants prefer shade to sun. Most ferns do best in acid soil, such as that under a tree with acid leaves like oak; but a few prefer the alkaline soil found over limestone rocks or at the base of a masonry wall.

Yet a summer shade garden need not be exclusively green. There are shade-tolerant foliage plants such as caladium and coleus whose leaves are streaked, stippled or otherwise marked with contrasting colors. And hostas, astilbes, hydrangeas, day lilies and summer sweets brighten the shadows with their summer-blooming flowers.

Shaded from the midsummer sun by the wide-spreading branches of Douglas fir trees, Sargent hydrangeas exhibit their clustering white and blue flowers. The shrubs receive up to four hours of filtered sunlight a day.

A grass path meanders through the green-on-green tapestry of a shade garden containing more than 60 species of ferns, including a feathery shield fern (lower right). The glossy shrub at left is a rhododendron.

Pink spires of Chinese squill, a summer-flowering bulb, create an elfin forest of bloom in the shade of high-branching trees. The background plants are azaleas, massed for a display earlier in the spring.

Stone steps lead into an all-green garden that mimics the forest floor. Epimedium softens the steps, Clematis sheathes the base of the tree and a feathery white pine seedling and ferns add textural variety.

Autumn's advance into winter

When the leaves on the shade trees assume their autumn hues, so do the plants beneath them. The berries of maple-leaved viburnum ripen to purple-black and its leaves turn red; the leaves of withe rod, another viburnum, become deep scarlet. More color appears in fall-blooming plants like the evergreen Darley heath, whose lilac-pink flowers appear in the fall and sometimes bloom through the winter. Fall-flowering anemones put on their annual display, and so do such bulbs as aconite and the autumn crocuses. In winter, attention shifts to the evergreens—hollies, hemlock, mountain laurel, winter creeper, yew. To ease this late-year transition, some shade gardens include evergreen and deciduous versions of a single plant, like azalea or blueberry, growing side by side, as in the garden opposite.

Set briefly ablaze by a thin autumn sun shining through the bare branches of an oak tree, a young threadleaf Japanese maple momentarily dominates a clump of azaleas and two mossy rocks.

Deciduous Japanese azaleas, chosen for their brilliant autumn foliage, sparkle among evergreen azaleas and rhododendrons. The orange-red leaves in the foreground are those of a Weyrich azalea.

A red-berried Perny holly and a Japanese andromeda tipped with puffballs of snow are among the evergreens growing beneath

the pendulous branches of tall deodar cedar trees. They form a shade garden that screens out the nearby road even in midwinter.

Working with shape, texture and color 2

Many shade enthusiasts think of their gardens in terms of four layers: the shade canopy of tall or medium-sized trees, the smaller trees that make up what is called the understory, the large or small shrubs and, finally, the much smaller plants and ground covers. Your garden may have more or fewer layers. But whatever the number, a shade garden that does not simulate a patch of natural wilderness requires a well-developed design. With it, you can achieve both variety and harmony, in mid-January as well as in mid-July. Without a design, your garden may stray across the line from "muted" to messy—or monotonous.

Within the four-layer framework, expert shade gardeners seek to coordinate the form, texture and color of plants and other garden materials to create an attractive and coherent unity. One oak-shaded suburban garden, for example, includes nothing more than a few moderate-sized sorrel trees, a decorative row of two different kinds of azaleas, and a broad bed of periwinkle (also called creeping myrtle) surrounding a small terrace. The garden is deceptively simple—but it has enough variation of forms, textures and colors to keep it interesting.

Form, the overall shape, is a plant's most noticeable characteristic. Plants may be round, columnar, vaselike, pyramidal, weeping, spreading or creeping, in varying degrees of symmetry or irregularity. Unless you are willing to spend many hours pruning plants into artificial shapes, select those that will have the shape you want when they are fully grown. The vertical lines of such plants as arborvitae or the columnar yews, for example, provide very strong accents that heighten and narrow a given space—one effect you may wish to create. A dogwood, on the other hand, with its planes of spreading branches, establishes a definite horizontal line, as do most ground covers; these spreading forms emphasize breadth and spaciousness. Because weeping or arching plants lead the eye in a graceful curve

Like a gently flowing brook, a Japanese grass, Hakonechloa macra variegata, cascades past a rocky outcrop and the silhouette of a large Japanese andromeda to create drama in a corner of a shade garden.

back toward the ground, shrubs such as arching leucothoës are often used to taper and finish the ends of shady borders. Most plants are rounded, a restful form that adapts well to mass compositions. You might echo the rounded shape of a white oak tree with an underplanting of rounded skimmias or sweet daphnes.

USING THE UNUSUAL

While the repetition of forms contributes greatly to the overall unity of the design, plants whose shapes are unusual or arresting, such as a weeping dogwood or a leather-leaved mahonia, can inject the note of interest that keeps a garden from boring the viewer. But these distinctive shapes should be used sparingly—as should strong pyramidal or columnar forms—to avoid a jumbled and distracting composition. Also valuable to the gardener are plants that will assume a desired shape as they grow and mature. Stephanandra, a creeping shrub with deeply lobed leaves and strong roots that can anchor a slope, is especially admired by one gardener because it forms dense mounds two to three feet high. "If I want a hump or bump some place," she says, "and there's no rock handy, I call on stephanandra and the problem is solved."

The second element in the quest for an interesting design for your shade garden, and perhaps the most difficult to utilize effectively, is texture. A catawba rhododendron, with large, widely spaced leaves, is an example of coarse bulk in a plant, while a

PLANT SHAPES: GRABBERS AND SOOTHERS

ROUND SPREADING OVAL PYRAMIDAL COLUMNAR

In a shade garden the silhouette of a plant can be especially important. Lacking the contrasts of sunlight and shadow on its foliage and the impact of differences in color between foliage and flowers, shape may be a plant's major contribution to the garden's design. But shapes differ in the visual effects they evoke. Spreading, round and oval forms are restful, leading the eye horizontally, in its normal direction of movement. Pyramidal and columnar forms are more arresting; they attract and hold the eye. It is usually best to use these vertical shapes sparingly, as accents; otherwise they will throw the garden out of balance.

Japanese snowbell is delicate and fine-textured. But texture is a complex quality. The same plant may sometimes seem coarse or fine, solid or airy, closer or more distant, depending on a number of different factors. When it is viewed near at hand, a plant derives its texture from the size and surface quality of the leaves themselves and from the spacing of the leaves and twigs. From a distance, however, texture becomes a matter of the play of light and shadow on the leaves and the entire plant. Smooth leaves reflect light while velvety leaves do not; the latter appear to be darker and more distant. Plants such as aspens, whose leaves are borne on long stems and flutter airily in the breeze, seem to be lighter and finer textured than azaleas or laurels, whose leaves are more firmly fixed on short stems. But even a fine-textured hemlock will appear thick and heavy if it has been sheared, because shearing eliminates the play of shadows on the surface of the plant.

The juxtaposition of various textures can create intriguing optical illusions in your garden, making a small area seem larger, or giving an impression of unevenness to a level surface. Because fine-textured plants seem to recede, while coarse-textured ones appear nearer at hand, you can add depth to a grouping in a narrow bed by placing large-leaved galax in the foreground, for example, smaller-leaved, medium-textured hypericum behind it and fine-textured pachistima to the rear. Or, by judiciouly spacing lacy plants such as ferns or lily-turfs, you can evoke a light and airy atmosphere in the confines of a small walled garden.

MANIPULATING SPACES

As with form, a certain restraint in the mixing of textures is necessary. Using too many different textures or combining contrasts that are too abrupt will produce a garden as disquieting as a shirt made of burlap and lace. Gradual texture changes, on the other hand, lead the eye comfortably from one area to the next, a perceptual movement that adds life and sparkle to any garden. In moving from finer to coarser textures, one rule of thumb is that the leaf size of a plant should be no more than double that of the plant that precedes it. Keep the texture of the plants appropriate to the size of their surroundings; plants that are grouped around a small rock outcropping should be fine textured to avoid overwhelming the rock. On the other hand, a bank of heavy, large-leaved shrubs such as rhododendrons, mahonias or hollies would be effective planted at the border of your property, where a stand of wispy witch hazels would seem lost.

Closely related to texture, and equally complex, is the matter of color. It is influenced by the reflective quality of the surface, by the color of nearby objects and plants, by shadows in the garden and by

A SPLASH OF COLOR

the quality of light. In the shade, the gradations of blue, violet and green appear darker than they would in bright sunlight, while the warm reds, oranges and yellows are much less affected by the dimness. A yellow forsythia or winter jasmine in the dappled shade of early spring may prove very arresting to the eye, while a cool blue hydrangea or bluebeard may all but disappear in deeper shade later in the season.

AVOIDING DISHARMONY Warm colors—like coarse textures—tend to seem closer to a viewer, while cool colors tend to recede. With a deft touch, any of nature's colors can be combined successfully, but it is also possible to strike some very discordant notes with flowers. If, for example, you plant half a flat expanse of your garden with periwinkle, which bears lavender-blue spring flowers, and the other half with moss phlox bearing bright pink spring flowers, the result may be an uneasy imbalance. The warm pink will overwhelm the delicate blue and capture most of your attention.

Although for much of the year the predominant color in a shade garden is green, this hue ranges from the deep green of such ground covers as English ivy through the smoky gray-green of dead nettle to the soft yellow-green of an Emerald 'n Gold euonymus. And if the plants are evergreens, all these different greens can contrast with the brilliance of autumn foliage on the canopy trees overhead, or

PLANT TEXTURES: COARSE OR DELICATE

Seen close up, a plant's texture is determined by the size, shape and surface of its leaves. A plant with large, shiny leaves (right) will appear coarse-textured while one with small, slender leaves (left) will seem delicate. At a distance, however, it is overall density that counts. A feathery hemlock will look heavy and solid, while light filtering between the branches of a rhododendron will change its apparent texture from coarse to fine.

with the bare branches of a red-twigged Siberian dogwood in winter, or with the ephemeral blooms of wildflowers in spring. Try to visualize the colors that will be juxtaposed at any given time, including the color of nearby buildings and other structures; careless planting without forethought can result in some uncomfortable color clashes. One shade gardener found that some treasured red azaleas, when they bloomed, made a shocking combination with a nearby brick wall. Her solution was to cover the wall with moss. You can use color to unify a combination of plants that contrast in form or texture or to differentiate among plants of similar form or texture. Plants that have variegated foliage, such as hosta, coleus or caladium, and plants with white flowers can brighten an otherwise solid expanse of green.

Form, texture and color are all qualities of the disparate parts of your shade garden. Now you must consider how to fit the parts together into an overall design. Your plan should evolve naturally from what one landscape architect calls the "genius of the site." This is the sum of all the topographical characteristics that make up a particular location. You will want to pay special attention to the quality of shade, be it deep, medium or intermittent, and to keep in mind how the area will be used. Will you want to sit in the shade, walk around in it, play in it—or will it be primarily viewed from indoors? Does the area include utilitarian items such as garbage cans, a laundry line, a compost pile? Do you wish to frame a pleasant view, or block noise from a busy street? Finally, does your shady area lend itself to the symmetrical lines of a formal arrangement, or do rock outcroppings and other irregularities of the site call to mind a more natural design?

Any successful grouping of plants will have balance. This does not mean that it must be symmetrical, although it certainly may be. But the composition should impart a reassuring sense of equilibrium and stability without seeming lopsided. In a formal composition, each element has its mirror image, but an informal or asymmetrical arrangement achieves balance in a more subtle manner. Because its pyramidal form is so emphatic, a single Carolina hemlock, for example, has enough visual weight to balance a group of several spreading English yews. Or if a planting on one side of a walkway is made up of three yews with dark green foliage, you can offset their heaviness with a small variety of lighter-foliaged false cypress, so long as you plant five or six of them.

While balance gives unity to your design, focus and accent are needed to create a sense of vitality and movement. Accents provided by contrasts in size, texture, form or color will rescue a garden from

A SCHEME THAT SATISFIES

monotony. For example, the juxtaposition of feathery ferns will set off the round leaves of galax or evergreen ginger, while small clumps of hostas with white-edged leaves can enliven a border of rhododendrons when they are not in bloom. But if you try to combine two redbud trees, three large azaleas and a perfectly symmetrical Carolina hemlock in one cramped corner of your garden, you will create a horticultural three-ring circus.

PICTURE WITH A POINT

A focal point is the circus master that tells you what is more important and what is less so by making one plant (or one group) dominant. This plant or group will be the first thing the eye lights on and will be the element around which you design a given area of the garden—or perhaps the entire garden. Handsome, distinctive plants that perform this function are called specimens. A gracefully proportioned dogwood, a fine sorrel tree, a weeping hemlock—any one of these might be suitable. Once you have obtained the specimen, other shrubs and ground covers can be added to serve as companion pieces or background.

Underlying both balance and focus is the important consideration of scale in your design. Plants should seem appropriate to each other and to their location in the garden, and this usually depends on their relative sizes. A 15-foot hemlock tree rearing up from the center of a cluster of small azalea bushes will seem rudely out of place. Scale has been called a device to evoke emotion. Intimate scale, in which something is smaller than expected, can be amusing

Shade gardeners prize caladiums for their decorative heart-shaped leaves, which brighten the shadows with markings of pink, red, green and white. In South American jungles they are cultivated as food—when cooked, the poisonous roots are edible.

or can make you feel important; monumental scale has exactly the opposite effect, while normal scale is reassuring—because everything is the expected size.

Keeping plants in proper scale with one another and with your house requires periodic reassessment of the garden. Plants do get bigger, changing the effect of a grouping. Although it is generally wise in the long run to space plants according to their mature size, you may not want to wait that long to achieve an attractive design. You will simply have to be prepared to shift plants around when the time comes. "My biggest problem is crowding," remarked one shade expert about a particular group of plants in his garden. "Those two dogwoods were fine together, but now they've grown too big, and one of them will have to go."

Although this gardener has more than enough room in which to maneuver his plants, the principles of scale, focus and balance are even more indispensable to the creation of well-designed small gardens. Narrow city lots surrounded by tall buildings offer shade gardeners a special challenge. Not only is the shade likely to be deep and the air that is confined by the buildings to be stagnant and polluted, but compacted city soil is often exhausted of nutrients. Still, a good garden is possible if the soil is prepared with care (Chapter 1). There is not much you can do to alter the quality of light and air, so the plants you choose will have to be tough enough to survive. English ivies and ground covers such as ajuga and

CHALLENGING THE CITY

The coleus, popular with shade gardeners since Victorian times, is often called simply The Foliage Plant. Its color-splashed leaves of red, pink, yellow, white, green or burgundy make a fine showing in a shady border. In winter, coleuses can be grown indoors.

moneywort have been found to do well under these adverse conditions, as have shrubs such as leucothoë and Japanese andromeda. Some city gardeners buy potted plants and sink them in the ground for the summer. Impatiens, caladiums and wax begonias can be handled in this way. Whichever route you take, spraying the plants' leaves regularly and often with a garden hose will remove soot and other residues of air pollution.

WAYS TO FOOL THE EYE To make the best of the dimensions of your garden, consider the effects you can create by choosing different forms and by juxtaposing various textures and colors. Strong vertical shapes emphasize the narrowness of a space, so there you will want to concentrate on spreading, shade-tolerant plants such as dogwoods and low-growing shrubs such as spreading English yews or sweet daphnes. Planting coarse-textured shrubs at the far end of the garden will bring that boundary visually closer to the house. Make the garden seem wider by projecting one or two plantings inward from the sides of the lot, thus interrupting a direct view to the back of the property. One of these screens might be an ivy-covered trellis or a stand of feathery bamboo, behind which a visitor might discover a bed of hostas or a small rock garden. Although rock gardens are often thought to be dependent on sunlight, one of their great advantages is that they provide a cool, moisture-conserving area for plant roots. Given good drainage and soil that is rich in humus, many shade-loving plants such as ajuga, crested iris and the saxifrages adapt readily to a rocky setting.

Rock gardens also blend beautifully into the kind of woodland setting that is favored by those shade gardeners who are particularly

(continued on page 44)

Shelters made to cool the sun

"Oh for a lodge in some vast wilderness, some boundless contiguity of shade," sighed the English poet William Cowper. Many gardeners, sharing Cowper's sentiment, have built themselves outdoor shelters that screen the sun's rays. Two of the easiest shelters to construct are the pergola and the lath house. A pergola is a colonnade supporting an open roof of heavy parallel rafters. A lath house consists of lighter, often crisscrossed wood strips. The amount of shade cast is determined by the spacing of the strips. Both can be designed to stand alone in a garden or to cover a terrace or deck that adjoins a house.

By providing shade where none exists, pergolas and lath houses serve many uses. They offer ideal conditions for starting seeds, for propagating cuttings, and for hardening off young seedlings. They create a summer home for house plants that need protection from full sunlight, such as tuberous begonias, fuchsias, impatiens and ferns. And their slatted, shade-giving roofs offer gardeners a restful retreat from the noonday sun.

A redwood pergola ends in a small lath house which provides shade for house plants, including begonias and orchids.

A California lath house, displaying traditional latticework, doubles as an entertainment area and a home for ferns, azaleas, palms and a fig tree. Its roof can be removed in sections.

This contemporary redwood lath house has two waist-high shelves for storing and tending plants. By filtering sunlight, the laths help to lower air temperature and slow evaporation.

The simple gridwork of a wide redwood pergola turns a deck into an extended living room. The parallel rafters run north and south so light and shadow are constantly in motion below. In the foreground is an evergreen pear tree.

fond of wildflowers. Many gardeners, in fact, when adjusting their plans to suit a shady environment, find themselves increasingly interested in native plants. Some choose to create a woodland that uses only plants that are native to their particular section of the country; others enlarge their scope to accept plants from similar environments elsewhere in the world.

Under the first plan, if your wild garden is in the Northeastern United States, for example, you might limit yourself to trilliums,

WIDENING THE VIEW

To make a narrow city garden shaded by building walls seem wider, divide it into several small areas with plantings that run at right angles to the walls. Within each area, vary the treatment at ground level. Where shade is dense or soil is poor, pave with brick, flagstone or gravel. Carpet a less shady area with a ground cover or transform it into a rock garden. Give all plant beds curving borders to make the garden seem larger.

bloodroot, hepatica and wild ginger, along with laurel, wild azaleas and ferns. Under the second plan, you might add such non-natives as the epimediums (from Japan and Europe), sweet daphne (native to both Europe and Asia), the Asiatic primroses and any of a number of hostas (from China and Japan). In either case, whether you give over a major portion of the garden to wildflowers or use them as surprises tucked away in corners, your wildflower plantings will need soil that contains even more humus than the other shade gardens. And, depending on the region, you may have to add generous helpings of oak-leaf mold or peat moss to give the soil the acidity that most woodland plants require.

Soil is only one of the regional variations that can determine both the plants you select and the style of garden you create. Another obvious variable, of course, is climate. Rhododendrons, for instance, are good shade-garden plants in many parts of the country. But in the South and Southwest many species do not grow well even in the shade, simply because of the heat. Determined rhododendron fanciers in areas where shade trees are at a premium will sometimes construct lath houses and arbors *(page 40)* simply to shield their favorite plants. Even where some natural shade is available, many warm-region gardeners prefer the textural variety and distinctive forms that are provided by man-made structures, where hanging containers of ferns and other shade-loving plants can create a cool setting on a summer afternoon.

Two other regional aspects to consider—and they are intimately related to each other—are the general appearance of your landscape and the kinds of trees that form your shade canopy. These determine the kinds of plants you can grow in your garden and whether the garden itself will seem integral to the region. The predominant plants in mountainous regions, for example, are conical or pyramidal evergreens. In the flatness of the Great Plains, tall vertical lines are often lacking. The mood under high-branching moss-draped live oaks in Georgia is entirely different from that found under a Douglas fir in the Pacific Northwest. The forms of these trees will influence the shapes of the plants you set under them in the same way the quality of their shade will determine what plants will grow there.

Whatever the location or size of your garden, applying principles of design to the selection of plants and their placement will greatly enhance your pleasure in your garden in the shade. As one visitor to the garden of the French impressionist Claude Monet remarked, "Everything is prudent, even the exuberance; everything is prepared, even that which seems wild."

COMPATIBLE LANDSCAPES

A palette made up of tranquil greens 3

The pleasing look of a soft expanse of lawn accented by the darker tones of a boxwood shrub, or the crisp appearance of tough, glossy holly against a sweep of pachysandra ground cover suggest the many possibilities of an all-green shade garden. Green is rich and varied in its shades and tones. It can veer toward yellow, giving an impression of warmth, or toward blue, which seems cool. There are bottle greens, olive greens and many other shades. And foliage texture provides a widely varied set of gradations, from hard and shiny to soft and velvety, and from smooth as glass to rough as an old board.

Experimenting with the gamut of possible combinations of color and texture constitutes one of the great joys of shade gardening. This is especially true if the garden is in deep shade. Where no direct rays of the sun ever penetrate, few plants will bloom, and the potential of green as a color scheme becomes most apparent and important.

"There is a tremendous number of shades of green; the range is almost endless," says one shade gardener. "You may never realize it until you see a garden like mine where it is all spread before you." There, within his view, are dwarf weeping hemlocks cascading over rocks, their dark green needles looking almost light against the blackish-green foliage of nearby yews. The heart-shaped pale leaves of wild ginger stand out in bold relief against the bright green stars of soft hairy cap moss. Spiky grasses and bamboos, ivies and ferns add their varied shades to the palette. Without the intrusion of the sun's harsh light, the perfection of each plant is clearly revealed.

This is a kind of beauty that those master gardeners, the Japanese, have long appreciated. They particularly admire the subtleties that are possible through the artful and imaginative use of foliage alone—the hallmark of sophisticated shade gardening.

Starting at the lowest level of garden vegetation, there are numerous ground covers that grow very well in the shade, including, perhaps surprisingly, certain varieties of lawn grasses. No grass will

A prostrate Canada hemlock, trained on stakes, rises like a shaggy figure in the midst of this garden composed entirely of richly textured foliage. Towering oak trees admit intermittent sunlight.

grow in really dense shade, such as that under low-branched evergreens or shallow-rooted, heavily foliaged Norway maples. But with the right kind of grass and the right care, it is possible to develop an acceptable lawn in medium shade. The task is even simpler, of course, if there is some intermittent sunshine, as in dappled shade.

LAWN CONSIDERATIONS

This possibility of using some grass appreciably widens the range of garden designs. Grass is very practical—no other ground cover will take so much trampling without damage—and it adds one more unique texture to a shade garden. Grass that grows in the shade needs mowing less often than that in the sun, and it harbors fewer troublesome weeds—crab grass, for example, will not grow at all in the shade.

With reduced access to light, shaded grass may fail to develop strong, deep roots. Good soil preparation, adequate fertilizing and high mowing with sharp blades are absolute requisites. But first you will need to select a kind of grass that is at home in the shade. The one you choose will be partly governed by where you live—in the Northern part of the United States or Southern Canada where cool-region grasses grow best, in the South where warm-region grasses are preferred, or along the border between the two regions.

In the North, the first-choice shady-lawn grasses are the fescues, principally red fescue. They grow well even when neglected, needing only modest watering and fertilizing. Red fescue is a fine-textured grass with needle-like leaves that conserve moisture, enabling the plant to survive droughts. In a hot, dry summer, however, it tends to become dormant and turn brown. If that happens it should be left alone; watering and fertilizing will not only fail to revive it but will actually weaken it. The grass will recover with the return of rain and cool temperatures. Chewings fescue is another variety that performs well in the shade, but for a lawn avoid tall fescue, a coarse grass that grows in clumps.

GRASSES FOR THE SOUTH

In warm regions, a good shade performer is St. Augustine grass. It does particularly well in humid regions and along the Gulf Coast—it is tolerant of salt—and it develops a thick, somewhat coarse turf that discourages the intrusion of weeds. Its major drawback is its susceptibility to chinch bug attacks, necessitating regular applications of pesticides. A more finely textured alternative is centipede grass, which is easy to maintain, although it does not tolerate foot traffic well. Many Southern gardeners with shade use zoysia grass, a slow-growing grass that in time provides a tough and attractive turf. Like the other warm-region varieties, zoysia is started with sprigs or plugs rather than seed, and it turns brown with the first frost, becoming green again the following spring.

Shade gardeners who live in the transitional area between the cool and warm regions, in a belt stretching through the middle of the United States, face a special dilemma. Their climate may be too warm for cool-region grass and too cold for the others. If you live in such a region, which of the varieties you use is likely to depend on characteristics of your garden that affect its microclimate—whether it is on a north- or south-facing slope, whether or not it is sheltered from wind, what its altitude is. Many shade gardeners in this region use zoysia grass, which is often offered for sale in the North even though it is primarily a warm-region grass.

All of the shady-lawn grasses need as much care as you can lavish on them. If possible, prune the trees to thin the shade canopy over the lawn area, removing lower branches. A substantial amount of effort is required to condition the soil directly beneath shade trees to ready it for grass. Spread a bale or more of peat moss—depending on the size of the tree—from the trunk out to five feet beyond the branch spread. To this add a copious layer of a turf fertilizer that is

CONDITIONS TO BE MET

All in the name of sphagnum moss

Sphagnum moss, a scraggly bog plant, is the basis of an invaluable soil conditioner for shade gardens. It is harvested and sold either dried or partially decayed. In its decayed form it is peat moss. However, sphagnum peat moss is often confused with other forms of sphagnum moss, as well as with peat that comes from other kinds of plants. Herewith are some definitions:

● *Dried sphagnum*. Most sphagnum is dried after it is harvested. It may then be chopped, shredded or milled. Dried sphagnum is marketed under a variety of names, including milled sphagnum, unmilled sphagnum, long-fibered sphagnum, green moss and sheet moss. Slightly antiseptic and highly absorbent, dried sphagnum is too expensive for use as a shade garden soil conditioner but is ideal as a medium for germinating seeds. It is also widely used for shipping live plants, for mulching and for rooting cuttings.

● *Peat*. The remains of any plant that has partially decomposed in a swamp, bog or other body of water and has been dug up and dried may be sold as peat. There are many different kinds of peat, including reed, sedge and sphagnum peat moss *(below)*. They vary greatly in their nutrient content and in their ability to retain water, so their use in shade gardens also varies with the specific needs for these characteristics. Most of the so-called Michigan peats are sedge peats. Examine peat packages carefully to make sure you get the kind you want.

● *Peat moss*. The peat derived from decomposed sphagnum moss outshines other peats as a soil conditioner for the shade garden. Its coarse texture lightens and aerates hard-packed clay soil under trees or near buildings. Its tremendous capacity for absorbing water—it can absorb 15 to 20 times its own weight—helps keep plant roots moist. Highly acidic, it is ideal for the many shade plants that have a natural preference for acid soil. Most processed peat moss comes from bogs in Canada and Europe.

strong in nitrogen (represented by the first of the three percentage numbers on the package); you will need at least 25 pounds of it around a shade tree 65 feet tall (the amount varies somewhat with trunk diameter and the chemical content of the fertilizer). Add ground limestone as well if the soil is acid, as it is likely to be beneath oak, beech or pine trees. Five pounds of ground limestone per 100 square feet should achieve the necessary correction in soil chemistry. Spread the limestone after you apply the fertilizer; if you reverse the order, the whiteness of the limestone will make it difficult to see whether or not the fertilizer has been spread evenly.

Mix these materials into the soil six to eight inches deep, using a sharp square-bladed shovel. This not only will loosen the soil but will destroy many of the small feeder roots of the tree near the surface. New feeder roots will replace them in time, but meanwhile the young grass plants will be able to send down their roots free of competition. After smoothing the surface, add a few additional pounds of fertilizer, then spread the grass seed or install sprigs or plugs. Keep the surface of the soil constantly damp until the new grass has become well established.

OFF TO A GOOD START   Fall is the best time to start a shady lawn, so the new grass will gain strength under the sun before the deciduous trees leaf out in the spring. Remove all fallen leaves from newly planted areas, raking

PREPARING SOIL FOR A SHADY LAWN

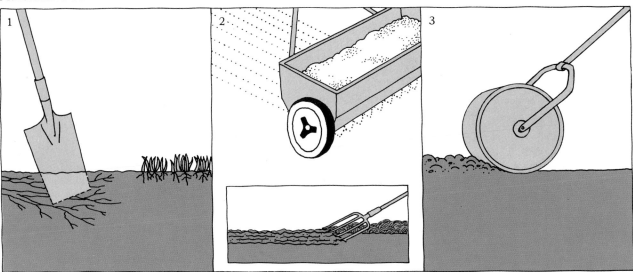

To prepare an area under a tree for shady-lawn grass, till it to a depth of 5 to 7 inches, using a spade to cut through the tree's feeder roots. Remove debris and rake the surface to even out high and low spots.

Dig in 2 or 3 inches of peat moss or leaf mold and add a nitrogen-rich fertilizer. If the soil is too acid for the grass you plan to grow, rake in a thin layer of ground limestone to neutralize the acidity.

Go over the entire area with a light, empty roller to firm and level the soil without compacting it. Make sure there are no low spots where water can collect and remain after heavy rains. Water with a fine spray.

very gently to avoid injuring tender grass shoots. Once the lawn is established, aerate the soil at least once a year, either by punching holes with a spading fork or by using a hand or mechanical aerator designed for the task. If you applied ground limestone at the time of planting, you will most likely need to repeat the process every three years, spreading the lime on top of the grass. The best time to do this is in late fall, so the lime can work its way into the ground through crevices caused by freezing and thawing, especially during late fall and early spring.

UNFAMISHED FESCUES

You might expect that after lawns are established in shade they would continue to need more fertilizer than those in the sun, for they compete with trees for nourishment. But surprisingly, fescues growing in a cool region need less than average feeding. Red fescue, for example, should be fertilized only in late summer—the main feeding—and again in the late spring after the soil has had a chance to dry. Red fescue should not be fed during the heat of the summer. Among Southern grasses, St. Augustine and zoysia need to be fertilized more often, in March, May, July and September. But centipede grass should be fed sparingly: a light application in spring and another in summer—no more. As for watering, the fescues relish dry soil and need little water to supplement rainfall. The Southern grasses need once-a-week watering throughout the summer. When

PLANTING GRASS IN A SMALL SHADED AREA

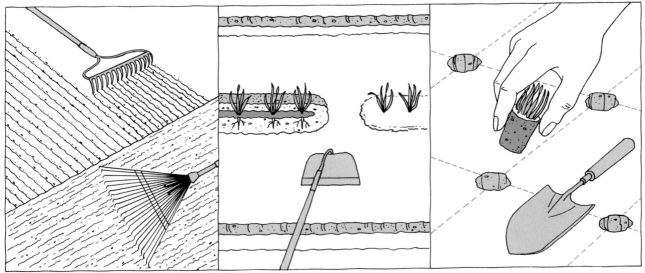

To seed, create shallow furrows with a rake (top). Broadcast seed lengthwise, then crosswise. Drag a leaf rake across the furrows (bottom) to barely cover the seed. Water thoroughly with a fine spray.

To plant sprigs of creeping grass, use a hoe to open furrows 3 inches deep and 8 to 12 inches apart. Set the sprigs 6 to 12 inches apart. Replace and firm the soil around each sprig. Water the area thoroughly.

To plant plugs of grass, mark off a grid with a rake handle using 6- to 12-inch intervals. Dig a hole at each intersection, fill the hole with water, then set in a plug. Firm the soil, and water thoroughly.

you water, soak the soil to a depth of at least six inches, applying the water slowly so none runs off.

Most shade grass should be mowed higher than its sunlit counterpart; it needs the extra leaf area to manufacture food. When you cut fescue, St. Augustine grass or centipede grass, set your mower two and one half or three inches high. Mowing it and the other grasses at this height reduces the need for watering and helps keep weed seeds from sprouting. If weeds do appear, pull them by hand; avoid chemical controls that might damage nearby shrubs or trees. Zoysia is an exception to the high-mowing rule; it forms a tight carpet and should be mowed at about one inch.

DELIGHTFUL DICHONDRA

There is one weed that many homeowners do not suppress because it has achieved respectability as a durable, attractive substitute for grass. This is dichondra, a low-growing round-leaved plant that flourishes in warm areas of the South and Southwest. Only a generation ago it was considered a noxious weed, but today at least half the lawns in the Los Angeles area consist of dichondra alone and many more contain a measure of it. It will sustain considerable foot traffic, though not enough to qualify it for playground use, and it grows very well in the shade. Indeed, it grows taller in the shade—up to six inches—and thus needs more frequent mowing. It is mowed the same as grass and must be watered often. So popular has it

HELPING GROUND COVERS SPREAD

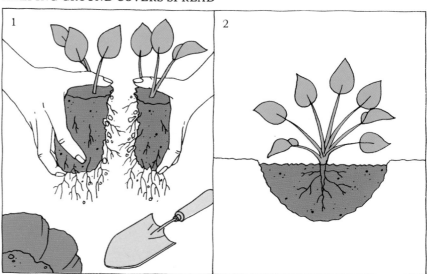

To divide clumps of shallow-rooted shade-tolerant perennials like hostas, dig them up in early spring and gently pull them apart by hand, keeping a few leaves on each segment. Or pry with a forked tool.

Prepare the soil for replanting by spading to a depth of 1 foot, mixing in a dusting of a root-stimulating fertilizer like 0-20-20 and 2 to 3 inches of peat moss or leaf mold. Replant, firm the soil, and water thoroughly.

become that it has achieved, for a weed, the ultimate accolade: many homeowners, yearning for a perfect lawn, go to great lengths to keep their dichondra from being infested with grass.

Dichondra is, of course, a ground cover, one of the most diminutive. Although many gardeners use ground covers because they will grow where grass will not, there are good reasons to think of them not merely as grass substitutes but as plants that can enhance a garden in numberless ways of their own. They fill awkward spaces, prevent erosion, form barriers, soften the lines of a path, edge a flower border, enliven a densely shaded area and provide a transition between shrubbery and grass, to list just a few of their uses. Many of them burst into bloom in the spring.

Once they are established, ground covers generally require little watering or fertilizing, and when they are fully grown they will actively suppress weeds. Although individual plants can be relatively expensive, many of them can be divided or propagated with ease. One suburban couple began planting their shady front yard with a few rooted shoots of periwinkle donated by neighbors. Within a few years, by dividing and redividing these plants, they had a flourishing bed 30 feet wide and almost 100 feet long and were giving away periwinkle shoots themselves.

Many ground covers will flourish in poor light. In deciding which ones to grow in a shade garden, you should keep several things in mind. First, although many ground covers are evergreen, others disappear in the winter, leaving a blank expanse that you may need to conceal with a mulch such as bark or buckwheat hulls. Second, because few ground covers may be walked on, such a bed is out of bounds for strenuous play. Third, combining different kinds of ground covers can provide pleasing effects, but beware of mixing low and tall plants—the low ones will be lost to sight.

Finally and most important, note that many ground covers will spread rapidly even in full shade. Depending on your needs, this characteristic may or may not be an advantage, so check the growth rate of any ground cover you are thinking of installing. If you want to cover a large area in a hurry, a rapid spreader like lamium, a handsome silvery plant also known as dead nettle, may be ideal; for a small space, choose a less enthusiastic grower, perhaps one of the epimediums. Most ground covers spread either by underground stems called stolons or by sending runners along the surface to root here and there. The latter are easier to control because the runners are visible. One underground spreader, pachysandra, is so noted for its exuberant growth that an old garden adage notes, "The first year it sleeps, the second year it creeps, the third year it leaps."

VALUABLE GROUND COVERS

SELF-MADE CARPETING

53

Keep in mind that while ground covers are to a large extent maintenance free, that blissful state of affairs is not achieved until the plants are well established. In the early stages, they must be fed and watered, and you must weed or mulch for two or three years before they are ready to block out other growth on their own.

THE THREE STAPLES

The most popular of the ground covers are Japanese pachysandra, periwinkle (also called creeping myrtle) and English ivy. The upright-growing pachysandra in particular is very widely used; it is evergreen and it actually prefers shade to sunlight—in full sun it is less vigorous. Periwinkle grows lower than pachysandra and its creeping stems have a softer texture. Not quite so quick to spread, it will withstand some trampling and will grow equally well in sun or shade, an advantage if you want to carpet an area that has both. Ivy, with its shiny leaves, spreads quickly with aboveground runners; more than 200 varieties are available, including some with leaves that combine green and gold.

Beyond these three staples there are several lesser-known plants that are just as dependable. One is the deep-rooted euonymus called winter creeper, whose vinelike stems make it seem like a slightly lighter version of periwinkle. Somewhat less adaptable to deep shade, it is nevertheless a vigorous grower in moist soil. Another good choice is one of the epimediums, also known as

AN IVY CARPET UNDER A TREE

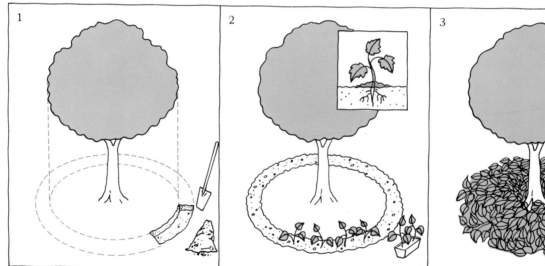

To cover the bare ground under a shallow-rooted tree with a rich carpet of ivy, first circle the tree with a trench, 6 to 12 inches deep and the width of your spade, just beyond the drip line of its branches.

Fill the trench with soil liberally mixed with peat moss or leaf mold and a phosphate-rich fertilizer. Plant rooted ivy cuttings 8 to 12 inches apart; press firmly around each cutting and add a mulch of leaf mold.

As plants begin to grow, direct stems toward the tree and pin them down with U-shaped lengths of wire (inset) to encourage them to take root. Keep the soil moist and free of weeds until the ivy is established.

barrenworts; these are tough plants that have light green leaves and display yellow, pink, white or violet flowers in the spring. Two very low ground covers with shiny leaves are galax, with foliage that is often used in floral arrangements, and wild ginger, whose edible roots were used as medicine by the Indians. Ajuga's coarser foliage provides a flat, dense matlike cover, as do the small, soft, round leaves of creeping phlox.

Sometimes called a ground cover but really in a class by themselves, the hostas are lush-looking plants that probably are the most dependable and intriguing shade-performers of all. Distinguished by wide, tonguelike, generally fluted leaves, they are also known as plantain lilies or funkias, and they are astonishingly varied. Of several hundred species, hybrids and cultivated varieties, many are available in America, and the list keeps growing.

Some hostas are only a few inches tall while others lift their foliage more than two feet up and one reaches five or six feet in height. With moderate light, they will bear blue, lavender, purple or white flowers between late June and September, but most gardeners grow them for their splendid foliage. Leaves can be solid green, blue-green, blue, yellow-green, striped or mottled and they may measure up to 18 inches long. Indeed, you could plant an entire garden of hostas and not lack variety. To top it off, they are virtually care free. Hostas are easily propagated by dividing clumps; one gardener purchased five plants for a dollar each and divided them each year. Three years later she had 70 plants.

Ferns make up another group of decorative plants that are useful in a fully shaded garden. Like hostas, most prefer a bit of sun, but some will grow quite satisfactorily in meager light, especially if the soil is moist and acid and is made porous by adding abundant amounts of peat moss or leaf mold. Ferns appear toward the end of spring, just in time to mask the dying blooms of early wildflowers.

For deep shade the most dependable as well as one of the most attractive is the Christmas fern, so called because it is evergreen and thus decorative in winter. A larger variety for deep shade is the interrupted fern with a stretch of virtually bare stem halfway down each fertile frond; it may reach a height of four feet and will tolerate dry soil if it is acid enough. Even taller is the cinnamon fern, whose sterile fronds are fernlike but whose fertile fronds consist of tassels of cinnamon-colored beads that contain the spores by which the fern reproduces. An unusual addition to a fully shaded garden is the Japanese painted fern, whose fronds, 12 to 14 inches long, range in color from gray through many shades of green to near-red. If your garden has a moist bank in dappled sunlight, you will want to try the

A HOST OF HOSTAS

FERNS OF MANY SIZES

55

elegant, lacy maidenhair fern, for it takes readily to cultivation.

Conversely, two otherwise attractive ferns are avoided by many gardeners because they take too readily to cultivation, spreading rapidly. One is the hay-scented fern—when crushed its fronds smell like new-mown hay—and the other is the New York fern. Of course, either of these fast-growing ferns may be useful in special situations—if you have a large area to fill, for example, or a sloping bank that needs anchoring.

A GARDEN OF MOSSES

The moist, acid environment that hostas and ferns prefer will also provide a good breeding ground for mosses, and many shade gardeners display moss collections with pride. There is nothing else in the gardener's world quite so rich and velvety as a carpet of moss. The 19th Century English essayist John Ruskin called mosses "meek creatures, the first mercy of the earth, veiling with hushed softness its dustless rocks." Once again, it is the Japanese who excel in their use. A common sight in their moss gardens is of groups of women on their knees, combing and weeding the tiny plants.

Mosses are surprisingly varied, with more than 23,000 species. One state alone, Michigan, has 400 identified species. Some mosses grow in the desert and others under water, and they include the familiar large sphagnum mosses that flourish in bogs. The kinds that grow in woodlands vary from minute organisms one sixteenth of an inch high that must be examined with a magnifying glass all the way up to the so-called tree mosses more than three inches tall. They carry such bizarre common names as fairy cups, hairy caps, knight's plumes and old man's beard. Because they often are found in the dankest, most densely shaded areas where nothing else will grow, they are equated by some with an unhealthy environment. But given certain conditions—usually just acid soil and enough moisture—they grow lustily and dress up any garden. Few nurseries sell mosses (except the sphagnum and peat used as soil conditioners), so the best way to acquire some is to seek them out in a wooded area that has an environment roughly comparable to your own. One moss collector calls moss "the one true do-it-yourself plant."

CLUMP OR CRUMBLE PLANTING

Mosses can grow either on rocks—they are featured in many rock gardens—or in the earth. In either case, they need a layer of muddy soil to hold them. There are two ways to plant moss, and you may want to try both. One is to plant an entire moist clump. The other is to dry the moss, crumble it with your fingers, and sprinkle the moss dust over wet ground. When you plant clumps, first turn the clump upside down and wash away the soil to expose the tiny hairs that are moss roots. Then flip the clump over and press it onto muddy soil, making sure no air is trapped under the clump and that all edges are firmly sealed with mud. The dry-and-crumble system takes longer to produce a new clump but is generally more reliable.

One moss gardener says that a sure-fire planting method is to put a handful of moss in a blender with a cup of buttermilk, mix well, then pour the mixture over the ground. The moss spores, she says, multiply in the buttermilk and produce a fine carpet in a few weeks. Another moss fancier uses a different recipe. She mixes a handful of crumbled moss with a can of beer in which two sugar cubes have been dissolved, then spreads the mixture liberally where she wants the moss to grow. This recipe, she declares, is particularly good for rocky terrain; the sugar helps the spores to multiply and the beer helps the moss to cling to the rocks.

Whatever method you use, keep the new bed moist until the moss starts to grow and wet enough thereafter to keep it green. It will notify you when it needs water by beginning to look brown and dry, but it will quickly turn green again when moistened. Covering a new bed of moss with damp cheesecloth will help keep it from drying out; the cover should be removed just as soon as the moss anchors itself. One further cautionary note: watch out for weeds. A clump of tufted moss provides an ideal breeding ground for such intruders, and there is no alternative to plucking them out by hand until no weed seeds are left in the soil beneath.

Above the ground covers, mosses and other low growths in a shaded garden you can develop an extensive collection of taller plants. If you grow wildflowers for their lovely spring blooms *(Chapter 4)*, their foliage in many cases will linger on into the summer for a time to add distinctive greenery, as will the umbrella-like leaves of May apple or the slender arching stems of bleeding heart. The rangy stalks and large, bright green leaves of Jack-in-the-pulpit are accompanied in summer by large clusters of berries that turn red as autumn approaches. Further splashes of color in an otherwise all-green garden can be provided by the large, flamboyant, heart-shaped leaves of caladiums, whose flowers are completely upstaged by their foliage; it can be red or pink and green, green and red with lilac spots, even pink and white with green ribs. A still different effect is produced by bergenia, a Siberian plant up to two feet tall with fleshy leaves that look like green table-tennis paddles.

FLAMBOYANT FOLIAGE

Leading anyone's list of shade-tolerant shrubs must be the rhododendrons and azaleas, particularly those that are evergreen. Both plants are members of the same botanical family, *Rhododendron*. Almost anywhere in the United States where the soil is at least moderately acid, these shrubs figure prominently in shade gardens, for after they complete their bloom in the spring, they are valued the

BROAD-LEAVED EVERGREENS

other 350 days of the year for their handsome foliage. For use in deep shade, the most reliable is the big *Rhododendron maximum* that can soar upward more than 20 feet and actually prefers shade to sunlight. But given its unwieldy size, you will want to investigate some of the hundreds of other rhododendron and azalea species and varieties that grow very well in shade. Foliage can range from blue-green to woolly beige to bronze-purple. However, precisely because they are shade plants, rhododendrons and azaleas are vulnerable to sun-scald injury in winter because harsh light streams through the deciduous trees that protect them in summer. With some species, you may find it necessary to provide winter shade, either with taller evergreens or by planting them near the north wall of the house.

LAUREL AND HOLLY

Equally appropriate for any shade garden is America's magnificent native shrub, the mountain laurel, with its graceful stems and glossy evergreen foliage. Its white, red or pink spring blooms will appear even in deep shade, though not as profusely as in sunlight. The hollies do well, too, especially Japanese holly, which has small leaves and resembles boxwood; it grows well in deep shade under punishing city conditions. Japanese hollies are not notable for colorful berries, but the hollies that are, particularly the fine varieties of English holly, will bear fewer berries in shade than in sun. And they will bear none at all unless you set out male and female plants within 100 feet of each other, at a ratio of one male to every ten females. In warm regions, shade gardeners favor camellias, whose dark, shiny foliage remains after the spectacular blooms have faded. Camellias require shade protection, at least from the midday sun.

PREVENTING WINTERBURN

1. *In winter, shade-grown broad-leaved evergreens often lose the protective cover of a leafy canopy and are exposed to harsh sun and cold winds, a combination that causes their leaves to wilt, curl and turn brown. To prevent this, plant them on the lee side of a house or a needled evergreen to cut the force of the wind.*

2. *To provide winter protection for a broad-leaved evergreen planted under a deciduous tree, construct a shelter of burlap stapled to posts. Make the shelter high enough to cut the sun's most intense rays, and place it on the windward side.*

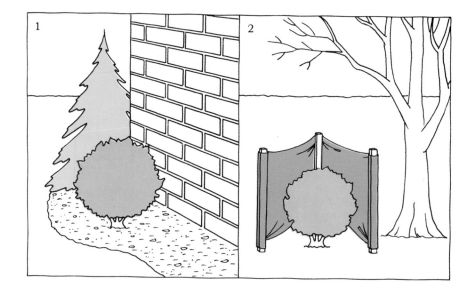

Of the needled evergreen shrubs, English and Japanese yews are perhaps the most dependable. They are both tolerant of full shade, but the Japanese yew is somewhat easier to grow. Some yews can reach 20 feet in height, and there are dwarf varieties that are only a few feet tall. The other needled evergreens guaranteed to grow well in shade are the Japanese plum yew and the hemlocks; among the latter are dwarf, prostrate and weeping varieties that are very ornamental in a shade garden. Most junipers, with blue-green needles, require sunlight, although some gardeners report success in intermittent shade with the very low-growing Blue Rug juniper and the vigorous, mounding Pfitzer.

To these familiar shrubs can be added a handful of lesser-known kinds that can enrich any fully shaded garden. Perhaps the most convenient is the drooping leucothoë, which will grow five or six feet tall if left unpruned but can live just as healthily as a ground cover cut back to 16 or 18 inches. Tolerant of bright sunlight as well as deep shade, it has lustrous leaves that turn bronze in autumn in sunny locations. For moderately small, narrow, glossy leaves you have a choice of sarcococca or the Nana variety of skimmia, while for coarser foliage three candidates are oak-leaved hydrangea and leatherleaf viburnum. Where the soil is quite moist, the sweet pepper bush will prosper; it is a delightful shade shrub which can diffuse a spicy fragrance over the entire garden.

To complete your green shade garden, you may want to add a few small trees that will thrive under the canopy of the larger deciduous trees. Dogwoods and Japanese maples can be handsome specimens, and some of the dwarf Japanese maples only a foot or so tall are exquisite. Some shade gardeners report success with some dwarf varieties of cryptomeria.

As the seasons change, many of these plants selected for a green shade garden will also change, providing a different color bonus for the autumn and winter. In the fall, for example, the viburnums turn pale pink, reddish purple or red, drooping leucothoë becomes bronze purple, oak-leaved hydrangea turns red or purple, winter creeper becomes purple-red and the burning bush lives up to its name by turning bronze, even in shade. Meanwhile the yews are decorated with red berries, as are partridgeberry, wintergreen, skimmia, holly and the dogwoods. In the winter, with both needled and broad-leaved evergreens remaining green, the viburnums and mahonias present yellow, red or bronze foliage, winter creeper retains its purple-red cast and the young stems of some kinds of dogwood shrubs are red. This display is still on stage in early spring as the first shoots of green announce a new shade garden year.

THE UNDERSTORY TREES

Varying the view at ground level

The shade that prevents a grassy lawn from flourishing offers its own reward—the opportunity to carpet the ground with a rich array of other plant materials, showing a surprising diversity of shapes and colors in both flowers and foliage. In using these materials, few modern gardeners are likely to want to duplicate the efforts of 19th Century gardeners, who painstakingly and literally re-created the patterns of Oriental rugs. But a ground cover can do for a garden what a good rug does for a room: carry the weight of the design, setting its mood, integrating its parts and underscoring its structure.

To perform this function successfully, the carpeting should be chosen for its own decorative appeal. Many ground covers stay green year round, and those that do not may keep their leaves, burnished with autumn color, all through the winter. Some bear flowers that may briefly dominate the entire garden design (*page 64),* and all of them are remarkable in one way or another for the texture, color or shape of their foliage—which may be small and dainty, crinkled or smooth, polished or velvety, monochromatic or speckled or striated with contrasting hues.

Your site and its climate must be considered in any choice you make, of course. Some shade-tolerant ground covers will best suit a Midwest environment with bitter winter cold, while others will add brilliant winter color to a hot and humid subtropical garden.

But a ground cover's success in the garden's design also depends on the contribution it makes, practical as well as esthetic, to the site. Some covers, like periwinkle and ajuga, do well even in deep shade, while others, like Baltic ivy, survive ice and snow. Pachysandra has such tenacious roots that it will cling to the slope of a steep embankment, as in the garden at right, while mosses will carpet the ground under trees where nothing else will grow *(page 66).* In some situations, the most effective ground cover is one seen close up; in others it is the overall vista that counts. Whether centerpiece or backdrop, the ground cover can often be the most significant element in the shade garden's design.

*A green expanse of pachysandra cloaks a
hillside shaded off stage by a huge oak and an
apple tree. The pachysandra's density
pulls together the garden's varied elements.*

Capitalizing on foliage alone

The size of the leaves of a ground cover, their texture and the subtle differences in their shades of green—these can be the raw materials for composing fascinating effects for carpeting the shade. By playing one kind of foliage against another or against the contrasting textures of rocks and trees, you can accentuate a garden's coolness, intensify its woodsiness, call attention to the role played by the pattern of a particular bark or a rock's striated surface. And though foliage is paramount, many of these carpeting plants also provide seasonal fillips of flowers and bright berries.

The sturdy leaves of goutweed, rimmed and streaked with white, form a dappled mat in front of a group of osmunda ferns, setting off the cool green of their graceful fronds.

The epimedium's decorative heart-shaped leaves, red tinged and deeply veined, lap one another gently, like feathers. In a mild climate, they will stay green all winter long.

Lamium, or dead nettle, sheaths the rough bark of a locust tree, its boldly marked leaves of silver and green standing out in sharp relief, as they do even in the dim light of deep shade.

The round, waxy leaves and orange stems of evergreen partridgeberry act as a foil for a small clump of club moss, or ground pine, whose stalks are covered with scalelike leaves.

The dainty leaves of creeping bluet, less than one-third inch across, form a velvety bright green mat around weathered granite steppingstones bordered with azaleas.

The leathery dark green leaves of wintergreen, and the plant's preference for an acid soil, make it an ideal ground cover under rhododendrons and azaleas, which have similar leaves.

63

An unrolling floral carpet

Though ground covers generally play a supporting role, for a brief time in the spring some of them flower so abundantly that they are the star performers of the shade garden. In the woodland garden shown here, windrows of wildflowers spread among the shrubs and trees, patterning the ground with waves of color as fresh and lovely as the colors in an impressionist painting. After the flowers have faded, the foliage will take over and the picture will change, becoming one of differently textured areas of green that flow together to give the garden a unified background.

A galaxy of spring-blooming wildflowers stretches through this garden as far as the eye can see. Prominent are creeping phlox in the foreground, white trilliums and the soft, creamy spikes of foam flower.

Underneath the foam flower's explosion of springtime bloom lie the mounds of decorative, deeply notched foliage that will carpet the ground in the summer, when the garden is wrapped in shade.

At least twelve kinds of moss of varying textures and tonalities carpet an area of this garden where the shade and shallow roots *of red oaks play host to little else. Some of these mosses appeared voluntarily; others were introduced from the nearby woods.*

Bright blooms for dark corners $\Big/_{\Big.}^{4}$

With the application of approximately equal amounts of verve and care, it is possible to keep virtually any plant alive in the shade. One Southern gardener defies convention and logic by growing roses under deciduous trees. They are tea roses that begin to bloom as early as February, before the trees have leafed out, while the roses still get sun. When the tree leaves do appear, flowering stops, but by then, she says, "I don't care—they have given me enough enjoyment." Such feats are not likely to be part of your plan, and there is no particular reason for them to be. There are a number of plants that flower freely and almost continuously with no direct sun at all, and many more put on the same kind of show in the sunlight that filters through trees or slants across the garden just a few hours a day.

Leading the list of these shade-tolerant flowering plants are two dependable tender perennials that are often treated as annuals in cold climates, impatiens and wax begonia. Impatiens, once familiarly known as patient Lucy, is by far the most popular of all shade plants, thriving under the most adverse conditions. Originally a rather leggy plant with modest blooms, it has now been hybridized into many varieties that bloom profusely and remain compact. These are easily grown from seed, producing flowers in three or four months. One Boston gardener who starts impatiens indoors from seed in February and transplants them outdoors in May, has a sea of pink, red and purple bloom in his garden by early July, though his city garden receives no direct sunlight.

Impatiens varieties come in a wide range of forms and colors, and with the introduction of New Guinea impatiens into this country, the selection became even wider. The New Guinea plants are sturdier than their more familiar cousins of American gardens, with thicker stems and bigger flowers, and some varieties have spectacular multicolored leaves combining red, yellow and green. Although they do not flower as abundantly as the better-known impatiens and

Astilbe spires contribute a burst of summer color to the dappled shade of a New England woodland garden. These hardy perennials need little coaxing to bloom year after year, but moist soil is essential.

are not as tolerant of shade, they provide valuable breeding stock in the development of new strains appropriate to shade gardening.

The other standby for shade, the wax begonia, also comes in an assortment of flower and foliage colors. The flowers can be pink, rose, red or white, and the foliage green or bronze; one variety has variegated leaves of green and white. A special virtue of wax begonias is that they bloom in both sun and shade, and so are valuable edging or border plants for a garden that stretches from a sunny area into a shady one.

A HANDFUL OF ANNUALS

In addition to these two plants, a number of annuals will bloom with a small amount of sunlight. One is browallia, which grows eight to ten inches high, with glossy foliage and blue, purple or white petunia-like flowers. Another is the somewhat smaller edging lobelia, a trailing plant that can be trained to cascade down slopes. Its flowers are somewhat similar to browallia's in color but they also come in pink and red. Ageratum will also provide its fluffy blue or white blooms in the shade, providing an interesting change of texture, and so will the pastel varieties of salvia, which actually grows better in shade than sun. The roster further includes sweet alyssum and baby-blue-eyes, and some gardeners would not be without nicotiana, the fragrant tobacco plant, whose red, pink and white flowers open at the close of day, when the light is fading.

Among biennials—plants that take two years to complete their growth cycle—foxglove and forget-me-nots are two likely candidates for shade gardens. But the list really lengthens when you add perennials. So many, in fact, are at home in the shade that you should plot their location with care, to take advantage of their color without inviting extra work: perennials tend to spread, and if they are planted too close to one another, they will have to be divided in a few years to avoid overcrowding.

SUCCESS WITH PRIMROSES

The favorite flowering perennial for shade is probably the primrose, which is frequently used in woodland settings and for bordering pools and brooks or lining paths. But primroses, as one experienced shade gardener says with a sigh, "are not easy to grow." They are natives of the Alps and the Himalayas where the air and soil are cool and moist. Summer heat plays havoc with their shallow roots unless they are kept well mulched. Similarly, in winter they must be protected from stinging winds. Pine boughs are excellent for this purpose, as are spruce and fir, and the primrose path is often the final resting place of the discarded Christmas tree.

If you want to try primroses, it is best to start with the varieties that are most flexible in their requirements. In most parts of the country the vernal primrose, from England, is probably the easiest

How to choose a shade-garden fertilizer

Fertilizers help restore depleted soil by adding necessary nutrients, especially nitrogen, phosphorus and potassium. These substances are particularly needed in a shade garden where trees often compete with smaller plants for nourishment. They can be supplied by organic or inorganic fertilizers, each of which has its virtues.

Organic fertilizers are made from the wastes or by-products of animals and plants. They release their nutrients slowly as they decay in the soil. Inorganic fertilizers contain man-made chemical nutrients. Soluble in water, these nutrients are quickly available to plants, but some of them leach out rapidly and can burn leaves and roots if not applied carefully.

Organic fertilizers are labeled with the name of the raw material and, like inorganic fertilizers, are marked with three numbers that indicate the ratio of nitrogen, phosphorus and potassium they contain (always in that order). In most fertilizer formulations the first, or nitrogen, number is the largest. This is because nitrogen quickly washes away, and also because it is the most important ingredient in plant nutrition: it stimulates stem and leaf growth.

Too much nitrogen, however, causes overly lush foliage and weak stems. It can also encourage foliage to flourish at the expense of flowers and fruit. Nitrogen is available organically in cottonseed meal, sewage sludge and dried blood.

Phosphorus, the ingredient indicated by the second number on fertilizer labels, promotes good root development. Phosphorus is released comparatively slowly, so there is less danger of excessive application. Organic sources of phosphorus include bone meal and rock phosphate.

The third major ingredient, potassium, improves the plant's general health. It strengthens roots and stems, making them more resistant to disease, drought and cold, and promotes better flowers and fruit. Organic sources of potassium include wood ash, rock potash and decayed leaves.

Nutrients needed in smaller amounts include boron, copper, iron and manganese. Deficiencies in these trace elements vary from one part of the country to another, and many fertilizer manufacturers accordingly provide regional formulations. Two organic sources of all the trace elements are dried blood and fish emulsion.

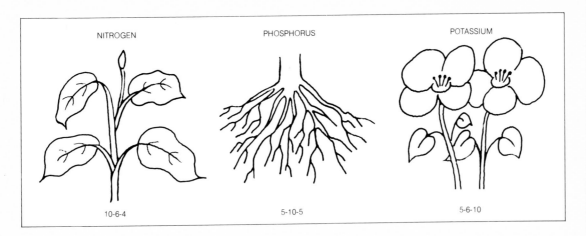

NITROGEN   PHOSPHORUS   POTASSIUM

10-6-4   5-10-5   5-6-10

to grow—followed by the polyanthus, or bunch primrose. The former has a single flower, usually yellow but sometimes pink, blue or purple; the latter puts out clusters of blooms on single stalks in a wide range of colors. Slightly more demanding are the Himalayan primrose, which bears lilac or mauve flowers, and the popular Japanese primroses, which grow two feet high and send up stems that are shaped like candelabra, bearing tier upon tier of white, purple and sometimes pink flowers. One Japanese variety, the Siebold primrose, does especially well in the eastern United States and is often planted in bog gardens.

The primroses generally bloom in the spring, with the earliest, the Himalayan, appearing in March; for the most part their flowering is over by July. Just when they are finished, another great family of shade-tolerant perennials comes into its own: the day lilies. Not true lilies but closely resembling them, these elegant plants with their arching stems have been garden favorites for centuries. American pioneers, who loved them because they required so little care, often grew them around their log cabins.

THE STATELY DAY LILIES

Originally day lilies bloomed only in midsummer and there were only sixteen kinds, all of them yellow or orange. Now there are hundreds of varieties—and an army of hybridizers, amateur and professional, is constantly engaged in creating more. Day lilies can be had in heights ranging from one foot to seven feet, with most of them hovering around the three-foot mark. Their flowers are one to ten inches across and come in every color of the rainbow except pure white and blue. Some varieties are bicolored or tricolored. The earliest of them begin to bloom in late spring and some varieties continue to bloom until the first frost. There are day lilies whose individual flower stalks contain as many as fifty buds; with each bud opening separately, one each day, the plant's total blooming season is fifty days long. There is even one variety of day lily that perversely blooms at night.

Almost as numerous as the day lilies are the irises. These plants are traditionally considered sun-loving, but a handful of iris species do very well in the shade. Chief among them is the dwarf crested iris, which blooms in the spring and is widely used as a ground cover because of its matlike growth. Another iris that tolerates shade is the evergreen roof iris, a native of China and Japan. And in the Pacific Northwest shade gardeners generally have success with three iris species that are native to that region—*Iris douglasiana, Iris tenax* and *Iris innominata.*

As the primroses, day lilies and irises succeed each other through the spring and summer, they are joined by the flowers of a number of other shade-tolerant perennials. In spring there are the blue bell-like flowers of Jacob's-ladder, the heart-shaped pink flowers of bleeding heart and the graceful flowers of columbine, whose hybridized versions come in pretty pastels as well as deeper colors like crimson. In early summer the feathery blooms of astilbe begin, lasting many weeks, and in midsummer the magellanica fuchsia is covered with small flowers in vivid combinations of ruby red, blue or purple. Then, finally, at the very end of the season—really the start of the season to follow—comes the amazing Christmas rose, pushing its saucer-shaped blooms through the snow in the dead of winter.

All of these annuals and perennials flower dependably when they are planted in open shade or in the on-again, off-again shade of gardens that get sunlight only briefly each day. But there is another category of flowering plants that do well in shade if they get seasonal sunlight during or just before their period of bloom. Among the most entrancing of these are the woodland wildflowers, sometimes called the "spring ephemerals" because they simply fade away when the trees leaf out.

One of the most popular of the woodland wildflowers is the trillium, a family of some 18 species with representation in most parts of the United States. Species seen most frequently in gardens are the white or snow trillium, the purple trillium called stinking Benjamin and the white to pinkish trillium called nodding wake robin. Other widely distributed woodland wildflowers are the bloodroot, Dutchman's breeches, foam flower, hepatica, May apple, Virginia bluebells, violets and shortia. If your shade garden has a moist soil, you might want to try marsh marigolds or the cardinal flower. And if it is downright boggy, two additional candidates are bluebeard and Jack-in-the-pulpit.

Many of these wildflowers are available from nurseries that specialize in them, and they can occasionally be found in large garden centers. Before you try transplanting them from the woods, check with your local horticultural society to find out which local species may be listed as endangered. In addition, if the woods are on private property, you need permission from the owner before you start collecting.

Woodland plants are best moved when they are dormant, so it is a good idea to identify them when they are in bloom, marking them with plastic markers, then return a month or so later to dig them up. Be sure to take plenty of soil around their roots, and keep the soil moist while transporting them home. Put them in the ground immediately, the very same day, in soil that approximates as nearly as possible that to which they were accustomed on the forest floor.

For most woodland wildflowers the ideal soil is one that is porous and filled with humus—more than is needed for other shade plants. It should be rich in compost and leaf mold, and it should also be well mulched, preferably with the leaves of oak trees. Zealous woodland gardeners develop a layer of what they call ground-litter—stray twigs, decaying logs, pieces of bark, fallen leaves or pine needles. This material helps to retain moisture in the soil and, as it decomposes, adds to the humus beneath. Given this kind of send-off and a little luck, the most finicky wildflower should, in a year or two, start blooming as regularly as a cultivated perennial.

EARLY-BLOOMING BULBS

Similar to these spring ephemerals in their need for seasonal sunlight is another group of plants, the hardy early-flowering bulbs that spend the winter outdoors. These too must have sun during and immediately after flowering to ripen leaves and restore the spent bulbs. Though not really shade plants, they are the stalwarts of many woodland gardens because their period of rest occurs in summer when the garden is in shadows.

Several kinds of hardy bulbs will bloom in a deciduous shade garden. Often the earliest to appear are the winter aconites, whose buttercup-yellow flowers push through the snow in mid- to late winter. They are particularly effective when planted in large numbers, as many as 25 or more bulbs together in a single drift of color. The winter aconites are followed by the better-known crocuses, especially the surprisingly varied species and hybrid crocuses. All of these multiply rapidly and may actually do better in woodland situations than in the open garden. Simultaneously with the crocuses (earlier in mild climates) come the snowdrops, whose tiny white flowers belie the fact that they are remarkably tough plants.

SPEEDING THE DAFFODILS

In the wake of these earliest flowering bulbs come the trout lily, also called the dog-tooth violet, the Siberian and Lebanon squills and glory-in-the-snow. But for many shade gardeners these are simply a prelude to the spring's star performers: the daffodils. Although daffodils normally demand sun, there are actually a few varieties, such as Arctic Gold and Ardelinas, that will tolerate some shade from trees. To hasten their time of flowering, some shade gardeners place them where the ground warms up fastest—on a south slope, for instance, or against a wall that gets reflected sun from the east or south. Finally, just as the garden is about to be overcast with shade, two late-flowering spring bulbs emerge, the tiny botanical tulips and the grape hyacinths—which are not really hyacinths at all (they belong to the genus *Muscari*, not *Hyacinthus*).

All of these spring-flowering bulbs require some additional consideration and care if they are to do well in the shade. They should not be planted under evergreens or against a north wall, where they will get no sun at all. Neither should they be planted near shallow-rooted trees like maple or beech, which will rob them of the moisture essential to their growth. On the other hand, you may have to guard against excessive moisture in the soil; bulbs do not do well in wet soil. It is a good idea to include a handful of sand in the bottom of the hole at planting time, to ensure good drainage. And last but not least, if you plant bulbs among thick-growing ground covers like ivy or pachysandra, make sure the plants will grow tall enough to reach through the ground cover to the light. Periwinkle, which grows more openly, is a safer choice for smaller bulbs. But the safest ground covers for these spring-blooming bulbs are the low-growing spring wildflowers that carpet the woodland floor—sweet woodruff, foam flower and creeping phlox.

All during the time the spring bulbs are decorating your garden, other bulbs are developing—varieties that bloom later and that do not require full sun to flower. They merely need sufficient light on their foliage in the spring to establish strong growth. There are, for example, a few lilies that do handsomely in the shade, though the family as a whole prefers sun. If they are used as shade plants, it is especially important to give them a rich, moist, well-drained soil. And paradoxically, because their roots do best when they are kept cool, they thrive under just the kind of thick ground cover that spring-flowering bulbs abhor.

The earliest is the storied madonna lily, which blooms in June. Later come three species native to North America: the Canada lily,

SHADE-GROWN LILIES

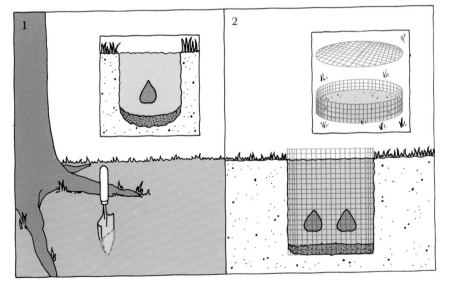

PLANTING AMONG ROOTS

1. *To grow hardy bulbs under a tree, dig holes 3 or 4 inches deeper than needed (Chapter 5). Put a handful of sand in each hole to speed drainage. Mix the soil with peat moss or leaf mold to lighten and enrich it, and partially fill the hole. Set in the bulb, right side up and at the proper depth, and firm soil around it, sprinkling in a teaspoon of bone meal. Water well.*

2. *To protect bulbs from burrowing animals, line the hole with ½-inch wire mesh at least 8 inches deep and extending aboveground an inch or two. Cover with another piece of mesh (inset), fastened with wire. In the spring, remove the cover.*

Turk's-cap lily and orange-cup lily. All of these bloom in midsummer, as do a number of hybrid lilies especially bred for their tolerance to shade, notably the Bellingham strain.

Along with these shade-tolerant lilies, you might want to try the oddly behaving hardy or autumn amaryllis, sometimes called the mystery lily. Its foliage comes up smartly in the spring but dies back in June as though the plant were dead. Then suddenly, in early August, a two- to three-foot-tall stalk appears, bearing a number of huge lily-like flowers.

Meanwhile, a second parade of blooms will have gotten under way. This one begins in early summer and runs through the fall, and it involves the tender bulbs, sometimes called spring bulbs because

TREATING LEGGY PLANTS

1. *To rejuvenate a many-branched shrub, like rhododendron or deciduous azalea, that has become leggy in shade, cut it back in three stages. Remove one third of its stems (the oldest ones) in late winter, cutting them off about 6 inches above the ground (blue). Remove more old stems in each of the following two winters. Fresh shoots will sprout from the stubs.*

2. *To rejuvenate an evergreen azalea, cut back long straggly branches to branching points in early summer (red bars), after the plant blooms. New branches will form just below the cuts.*

3. *To rejuvenate shrubs with canelike stems, such as forsythia and kerria, cut one third to one fourth of the old canes to the ground each year after flowering (red bars). New canes will grow in their place. Cut long new canes partway back (red bars) to slow growth and encourage branching.*

4. *To make a leggy nonwoody plant, such as a coleus, more compact, pinch off the tips of its branches to encourage new side shoots. For more abundant foliage, pinch off flower spikes as they appear, removing at least two leaves with each spike (red bar).*

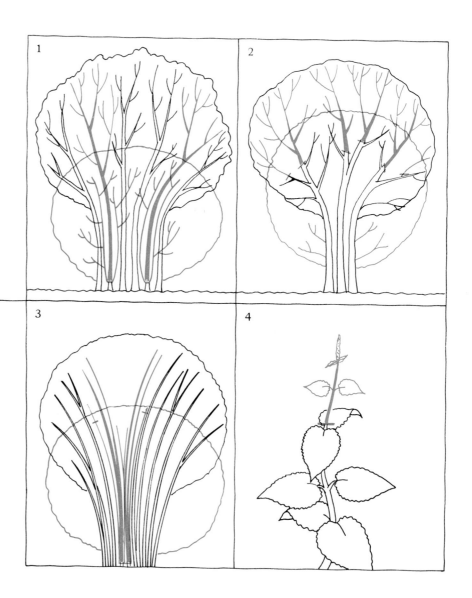

that is when they are put in the ground. In all except the frost-free parts of the country these bulbs are best started indoors and transplanted to the garden only when there is no further danger of frost. In the fall they must either be abandoned or dug up and moved into the house for the winter. Unlike their hardier cousins, the tender bulbs actually prefer subdued light to direct sun, which tends to burn their delicate foliage. They also need protection from wind. And, like hardy bulbs, they should never be made to compete with shallow-rooted trees.

The most spectacular of the tender bulbs is unquestionably the tuberous begonia, which requires meticulous care (*Chapter 5*) but rewards its caretakers with a profusion of flowers in an astonishing range of colors, sizes and shapes. There are also at least three other tender bulbs worthy of the shade gardener's attention. One is the achimenes, which flowers almost as abundantly as the begonias. It is an ideal plant for hanging baskets on a shady patio but it may also be massed in borders. Another is the calla lily, which grows best in wet soil and will even grow in a bog—although it will also do well whenever it gets enough moisture. The third is the diminutive zephyr lily, only 6 to 8 inches tall, delightful in rock gardens or naturalized in grass.

While all these various flowering plants—lilies, annuals, perennials and wildflowers—are brightening the shade with color, another display is often going on simultaneously around, above and beneath them. The trees, shrubs and ground covers that perform their greatest service as foliage plants may also periodically erupt into color. When the evergreen azaleas are in bloom, they are a world unto themselves. The forsythia and dogwood add splashes of yellow and white. And spring also brings, for example, the white flower clusters of viburnum, the silken white panicles of the fringe tree and the yellow blooms of Oregon holly grape.

In summer, the glossy abelia begins a period of flowering that will last until frost, and the heavenly bamboo—actually a member of the barberry family—is decorated with foot-long clusters of flowers. This is also the season of the hydrangeas, one of which, the climbing hydrangea, sends out its white blooms along stems that reach as high as 60 feet—given a tree to cling to. "That's my climbing hydrangea, holding up an oak," says one delighted shade gardener. For Southern gardeners, fall brings the pink and lavender flowers of the sasanqua camellia. And then, just before winter sets in, the common witch hazel bursts forth with yellow flowers as its foliage is also turning yellow. A shade garden may be predominantly green, but it need not be without a wealth of other colors.

TUBEROUS BEGONIA'S SHOW

AND SUMMER INTO FALL

Shadows that shimmer with color

"Nothing will bloom in the shade!" is a common complaint—but one that is far from true. Certainly, no gardener who has ever walked along a wilderness trail would be inclined to believe it. There, under the protective cover of leafy boughs, he might see hairy alum root, yellow loosestrife, clambering monkshood, Andrews gentian, cardinal flower and dozens of other plants generously unfurling their flowers. To supplement these native forest plants, for some three centuries horticulturists have been assiduously cultivating other plants that bloom well in the shade.

Impatiens, brought from Asia and Africa by adventurous sailors, was growing in English shade gardens more than 350 years ago. "This is a very tender plant, dying every yeare," wrote John Parkinson (1567–1650), King's Botanist to Charles I, "and must be sown carefully in a pot of earth, and tended and watered in the heate of Summer, and all little enough to bring it to perfection." Begonia and fuchsia, two other shade-tolerant favorites, made their way into British gardens by some roundabout route during the late 18th Century, having been discovered in Central America by a French monk, Père Plumier, some 100 years earlier. Fuchsia flowers were at first only shades of red, but over the years violet, orange, mauve, cream, white and pink hybrids have become available—more than 2,000 in all, many with petals of one color and backward-curving sepals of another. Hybridization of begonia and impatiens has also resulted in hundreds of exciting new varieties.

Add to these the shade-tolerant wildflowers that have also been cultivated for centuries—though more often for their medicinal value than their beauty—and it is clear that a wealth of bloom lies waiting to brighten any shady corner with unexpected color. Indeed these colors often seem more intense in the shadows. "Trilliums," observed English gardener and essayist Vida Sackville-West about one such wildflower, "have the advantage of lasting a very long time, which seems to be true of most woodland things, I suppose because they do not get burnt up by a hot sun."

Shaded in part by the feathery leaves of a tree fern, a begonia overflows its pot atop a stone wall. To shelter it from cold, its owner lodges it in a greenhouse in winter.

A tried-and-true trio

Three old-fashioned flowering favorites for a shade garden are impatiens, fuchsia and wax begonia. Creating continuous bloom from late spring until frost, these plants are unbeatable for infiltrating the garden's green with a splash of color. They can be the dominant element in a formal design, like the ring of begonias at right, which lies at the center of concentric circles of green lawn, shrubs and trees. Or they can be grown in portable containers to be used as colorful accents wherever needed. In frost-free climates, all three plants can be grown outdoors year round; but in the North they are treated as annuals or moved indoors for the winter.

Like leaping dancers, the pendant blooms of a fuchsia appear suspended in air. Each flower consists of four spreading sepals and four petals folded around a protruding style.

A pot of impatiens, bursting with pink flowers, lights up a stone wall shadowed by surrounding trees. Its neat, moundlike shape also makes it an excellent plant for edging walks.

Wax begonias surround a shaded pool and emphasize the garden's strict geometric plan. The plants were started in a greenhouse in midwinter and set into the ground in spring.

Cornered by two walls, impatiens in a terra-cotta pot softens the masonry surfaces with its mound of deep green foliage. At dusk, the flowers stand out like pinpricks of light.

The wild bunch

Most woodland wildflowers take naturally to dappled sunlight or open shade, though only a few, such as Jack-in-the-pulpit, will thrive in deep shade. Grouped together by their similar soil requirements, they return year after year, creating patches of color beneath the trees. In a wildflower garden, the less obvious the hand of man the better: the plants should be allowed to establish their own design. Start them off in a rich, porous soil containing abundant organic material such as peat moss or leaf mold to retain moisture. Each fall, let a layer of such ground-litter as fallen leaves and twigs cover them; the plants grow best when they go their own natural way.

A clump of snow trillium (foreground) and a carpet of moss phlox (left center) herald the spring in this woodland garden.

The pinwheel-shaped flowers of this wild geranium appear in late spring and early summer. In fall, its slender seed capsule cracks open like a crane's bill, tossing seeds at random.

The round, red-eyed flowers of a primrose rise from a careful replica of the moist forest floor. Like its many wild cousins, this plant does best in the open shade of high-branching trees.

Two pink lady's slippers lift their swollen pouches above a sea of white bunchberry. The lady's slipper, a wild orchid, needs a particular soil fungus to thrive.

*The intricate spotted flowers of a
hairy toad lily appear in early autumn.
A native of Japan, it grows to a height
of three feet under the intermittent
shade of high-branching trees.*

*A Jack-in-the-pulpit rears its
clublike spadix, or Jack, from a green-
and-purple spathe, the pulpit.
Neither Jack nor pulpit is the plant's
true flower; it is hiding inside.*

*A rough gentian unfurls its cupped
blue flowers in candelabra-like clusters
in cool, moist shade. The flowering
begins in late summer and continues
until midautumn.*

*The scarlet blooms of a cardinal
flower brighten a marshy woodland
garden from midsummer until fall.
Though hardy, the plant benefits from
a heavy winter mulch of leaves.*

An encyclopedia of plants for shade gardens 5

Shade varies from garden to garden. Often, it varies within a garden. There is the deep shade found under a low-branching tree or at the base of the north side of a high wall. No direct, and very little indirect, sunlight reaches these areas. Then there is medium shade, where no direct sunlight exists but indirect light is plentiful, such as under a tree with higher or more open branches. Finally, there is open or intermittent shade, where the sun may shine up to three or four hours a day, either all at once in a morning or afternoon burst of light, or cumulatively in the form of day-long dappled sunlight.

The following encyclopedia has been designed to help you select plants for the three shade categories: deep, medium, and open or intermittent. There are also specific references to the culture and characteristics of the plants listed. Some are notable for their foliage, others for their flowers, still others for their usefulness as ground covers. Many entries also provide climate zone numbers, keyed to a zone map of winter hardiness that appears on page 152.

Plants are listed in the encyclopedia by their Latin names, with common name cross references. In the case of maple-leaf viburnum, for example *(Viburnum acerifolium),* the genus name *Viburnum* is followed by the species *acerifolium,* a reference to the shape of the leaves. These Latin names are important in distinguishing this shade-tolerant plant from related species that require more sun. The same is true of other plants. Most irises, for example, require full sunlight—but the low-growing crested iris *(Iris cristata)* and vernal iris *(Iris verna)* thrive in open shade. Similarly, certain pastel-colored varieties of scarlet sage, such as Lavender Lace *(Salvia splendens)* run counter to the high-sun requirements of their species and perform best in open shade.

For quick and easy reference, the information described in detail in the encyclopedia has been put into a chart that appears on pages 149-151. The chart divides the plants into 11 categories, such as ferns, vines, ground covers and deciduous shrubs, for easier use in planning the various elements of your shade garden.

Among the visual delights of shade plants are Japanese andromeda's cascading flowers, epimedium's heart-shaped foliage, the striated leaves of hosta, plump hemlock cones and bright red chokeberries.

GLOSSY ABELIA
Abelia grandiflora

BLOOD-LEAVED JAPANESE MAPLE
Acer palmatum atropurpureum

A

ABELIA

A. grandiflora (glossy abelia)

Flowering profusely from early summer until late fall, abelia, a broad-leaved evergreen shrub, thrives in medium shade but needs some sunlight in spring to stimulate the development of flower buds. The plant's arching branches form mounds 3 to 5 feet tall and equally wide. Its glossy leaves, 1 to 1½ inches long, are coppery bronze when they first open in the spring; they mature to dark green by summer, then become red-brown in the fall. If temperatures fall below zero, the plant may lose its leaves or even die back to the ground, but if pruned hard it will usually survive and bloom the following summer. The bell-shaped flowers, ¾ inch long, are normally white flushed with pink, but a hybrid variety, Edward Goucher, bears pink-purple flowers, and there is also a white-flowering variety, Prostrata, that grows only 1½ to 2 feet tall and is valued as a ground cover.

HOW TO GROW. Glossy abelia is hardy in Zones 6-10 but should be planted in a location where it gets some protection from winter winds. It does best in a well-drained acid soil composed of 1 part leaf mold or peat moss to every 2 parts of soil. Though it will tolerate dry soil, keep the soil evenly moist and cool throughout the year, if necessary providing a permanent mulch of wood chips, ground bark or chunky peat moss 3 to 4 inches deep. Glossy abelias do not normally need fertilizing, but a weak plant may be strengthened by a light scattering of cottonseed meal or 10-6-4 fertilizer around its base in early spring.

Prune shrubs only to remove deadwood, and only in winter or early spring, because flowers develop on new growth. Rejuvenate old plants either by cutting shrubs to ground level or by removing the older stems in early spring. Propagate by rooting stem cuttings of new growth in late summer.

ACER

A. circinatum (vine maple): *A. palmatum* (Japanese maple); *A. pensylvanicum* (striped maple, moosewood, Pennsylvania maple)

These three small maples, among the most popular ornamental trees, flourish in open shade. In northernmost areas, they need good light for part of the day but protection from the hottest sun; in southern areas they grow best in continuous shade. These species range from 8 to 25 feet tall. Their pest-free foliage changes to brilliant shades of yellow, orange and red in fall before dropping from the tree.

Vine maple is a fast-growing round-topped tree with long, twisting branches that sometimes grow horizontally, trailing across the ground like those of a vine. It grows 15 to 25 feet tall and almost equally wide. Its leaves have seven to nine shallow lobes and are 2 to 7 inches wide; when young, they are tinted red, but in summer they turn green, then orange and red in fall. Before the leaves appear in spring, the tree bears dangling clusters of tiny red-purple flowers; in fall these are followed by red-winged seed capsules that remain on the branches well into winter. Also providing winter color are the many young red twigs that interlace the tree's bare branches. Vine maple's relatively low height and sprawling habit of growth suits it for use as a specimen planting on a shaded lawn or patio in combination with evergreens. Alternatively its branches can be trained to grow flat, as an espalier against a north-facing wall.

Japanese maples are slow-growing; most eventually reach a height of about 15 feet and are equally wide. But cut-leaved varieties, with deeply indented foliage, grow even more slowly, seldom becoming more than 8 to 12 feet tall and wide. Most kinds with conventionally shaped foliage have 2- to 4-inch leaves with 5 to 11 lobes; on cut-leaved varieties the leaves are 3 to 4 inches across. Although the original species has reddish leaves in spring, green leaves in summer and orange or dark red leaves in fall, the most popular Japanese maples have red leaves all year long. Recommended red-leaved kinds are the blood-leaved Japanese maple, *A. palmatum atropurpureum,* with dark purple-red foliage; Burgundy Lace with deeply indented red leaves on green stems; thread-leaved Japanese maple, a very slow-growing kind with deeply lobed leaves borne on drooping, gnarled branches; and Oshio-beni maple with deeply indented bright red leaves.

Striped maple grows 15 to 20 feet tall and spreads about 10 feet wide. Young trees and twigs have colorful white-streaked green bark. Their 5- to 7-inch leaves with three roundish lobes are red-tinged when they first appear in the spring, green in summer and bright yellow in fall. Both Japanese and striped maples are useful planted under taller trees or in the shade of high walls.

HOW TO GROW. Vine maple is hardy in Zones 6-9, Japanese maple in Zones 5-9, striped maple in Zones 3-9. All three thrive in moist, well-drained soil supplemented with leaf mold or peat moss. When growing a Japanese maple in its northernmost limits, choose a location with some protection from wind. Buy trees sold with their roots balled and burlaped in the original soil, and set them out in spring. Established trees normally do not need fertilizing, but a weak plant may be strengthened by spreading cottonseed meal or an all-purpose fertilizer around its base in early spring. No pruning is required except to shape espaliers.

ACONITE, WINTER See *Eranthis*
ADDER'S FERN See *Polypodium*

ADIANTUM

A. hispidulum (rosy maidenhair); *A. pedatum* (northern maidenhair, five-finger fern)

The maidenhair ferns thrive in every sort of shade, their delicate green fronds and lustrous brown-black stems suiting them particularly for planting among rocks or in woodland borders. Both of these species spread slowly on underground stems or rhizomes. The rosy maidenhair gets its name from the tightly wound leaf buds and young leaves, which are red in early spring, becoming green as they grow larger. The plant has erect 6- to 12-inch stems covered with tiny hairs and dark brown scales, from which several fronds branch out to a length of 8 to 16 inches. Each frond is lined with pairs of leaflets, ⅜ to ¾ inch long, bearing kidney-shaped spores along their edges. The foliage is evergreen.

Northern maidenhair's leaf buds are brown in early spring, its green winglike leaflets turning darker and becoming blue-green as they mature. The plant's erect 10- to 20-inch stalk divides into two stems that curve in opposite directions, parallel to the ground, forming a circle. The fronds radiate from this circle like fingers (hence the other common name, five-finger fern) and dip slightly at the tips under the weight of their leaflets. The northern maidenhair is a deciduous plant and bears concealed spores under the curled edges of the leaflets.

HOW TO GROW. Rosy maidenhair is hardy in Zones 9 and 10; northern maidenhair in Zones 4-8. Both do best in an acid soil composed of 1 part garden loam, 1 part coarse sand and 2 parts leaf mold or peat moss. The soil should be barely moist at all times, though less water is needed in winter. A mulch of leaves or evergreen boughs will help retain mois-

NORTHERN MAIDENHAIR
Adiantum pedatum

For climate zones and frost dates, see maps, pages 152-153.

SILVEREDGE GOUTWEED
Aegopodium podagraria 'Variegatum'

BUGLEWEED
Ajuga reptans

ture while protecting the less hardy roots of the northern maidenhair during winter.

Plant maidenhair ferns in spring, setting them 1 inch deep and 6 to 8 inches apart. Fertilize each spring by spreading bone meal around the base of the fern at the rate of 1 ounce per square yard. Remove leaves from rosy maidenhair when they turn yellow in fall and winter; remove dead leaves from northern maidenhair in early spring before new leaf buds unfold. Propagate by dividing rhizomes in spring as new growth appears or by sowing spores on a sterile, constantly moist surface within a week or two of their collection.

AEGOPODIUM

A. podagraria 'Variegatum' (silveredge goutweed, silveredge bishop's weed)

Whatever the quality of shade, open to deep, silveredge goutweed will thrive, forming a thick, summer-long carpet of coarse white-trimmed green leaves. The plants grow 6 to 14 inches tall, spreading rapidly on underground roots. Small saucer-shaped clusters of white flowers, ⅛ inch across, appear in midsummer above the jagged-edged foliage. In winter this foliage dies back to the ground. Silveredge goutweed grows so vigorously that it is best isolated in an area such as a strip near a wall where it will not crowd other plants.

HOW TO GROW. Silveredge goutweed is hardy in Zones 4-9 and does well in almost any soil. Plant in spring, spacing 6 to 12 inches apart. If foliage becomes unkempt, mow or trim close to the ground; new leaves will quickly appear. Propagate by dividing old plants in early spring or early fall.

AJUGA

A. reptans (bugleweed, carpet bugle, ajuga)

In any kind of shade, deep to intermittent, bugleweed forms a thick carpet of shiny crinkled leaves 2 to 4 inches long growing in low mounds no more than 6 inches tall. This perennial spreads so rapidly by surface runners that it may crowd out other small plants if it is not kept under control. The original species has dark green leaves, but varieties come with leaves that are purple *(A. reptans rubra)*, bronze *(A. reptans atropurpurea)*, purple splashed with red *(A. reptans* Rainbow), and multicolored marbled with creamy white or pink *(A. reptans variegata)*. All change to bronze in fall, and in cold zones the foliage dies in winter, reappearing in spring. Flower spikes of tiny blue, purple, red or white blooms rise about the leaves in late spring or early summer. Bugleweed is a useful ground cover under dense shade trees where few other plants survive; it can border a path, be tucked among rocks or be used as an edging.

HOW TO GROW. Bugleweed is hardy in Zones 4-10 in almost any soil, although it does best in rich moist soil. Set out plants in spring, spacing them 6 to 12 inches apart. Propagate by cutting off and replanting new growth that springs from the ends of runners.

ALYSSUM, SWEET See *Lobularia*

AMELANCHIER

A. canadensis (downy serviceberry, shadbush, shad-blow); *A. grandiflora* (apple serviceberry)

Downy and apple serviceberries, among the first trees to bloom in spring, thrive in open shade, although for the best flowers they need some sun during the period when their buds are swelling and opening. These fast-growing trees with slender branches usually reach a height of 15 to 18 feet, spreading equally wide, but may grow 20 to 30 feet tall and 10 to 15 feet wide. On the downy serviceberry, masses of

1-inch-wide white star-shaped flowers bloom on short spikes even before the leaves appear; they are followed in summer by tiny red-purple berries. The leaves, 1½ to 3 inches wide, are coated with soft gray down when they first unfold but turn clear green in summer and yellow, orange or red in fall. Apple serviceberry, a hybrid, has larger flowers; blooms 1¼ inches wide appear in late spring. Even in winter, the serviceberries are interesting for their soft gray bark. Downy and apple serviceberries are useful in woodland settings under taller trees, and their delicate open growth make them especially effective against evergreens.

HOW TO GROW. Both serviceberries are hardy in Zones 6-9. They do best in moist, well-drained soil enriched with 1 part leaf mold or peat moss to every 2 parts soil. Buy a tree with roots balled and burlaped in the original soil. In Zones 6 and 7, set out in spring; in Zones 7-9, plant any time from fall to spring. Established trees normally should not be fertilized, but a weak plant may be strengthened by dusting cottonseed meal or an all-purpose fertilizer around its base in late winter. Pruning is seldom required.

ANDROMEDA, JAPANESE See *Pieris*

AQUILEGIA

A. canadensis (American or Eastern columbine); *A. flabellata* (fan columbine); *A. hybrida* (hybrid columbine)

The dappled shade of a woodland clearing suits columbines perfectly, for that is their native home; they grow on dry slopes and rocky ledges wherever the climate is not too hot (daytime temperatures of 80° or lower) and are excellent plants for rock gardens and borders in open shade. The columbines are airy looking but sturdy; their unusual nodding flowers arch high above the deep-lobed leaves. The flowers, which bloom in late spring and summer, have five petal-like sepals on top of the true petals, which project backward to form hollow spurs ½ to 6 inches long that end in knobbed tips. The spurs contain nectar that attracts hummingbirds. The flowers are followed by seed pods that are divided into five segments. The seeds germinate readily.

The American columbine grows 3 to 4 feet tall and bears red and yellow flowers 2 to 3 inches wide. It is the parent of many hybrids. Fan columbine, a native of Japan, grows 1 to 1½ feet high; it normally bears lilac to white flowers, 2 inches wide, but there is a pure white variety, *A. flabellata alba,* and also a dwarf, *A. flabellata nana-alba,* the latter only 8 to 12 inches high. *A. hybrida* includes many varieties of columbine 1 to 3 feet high with flowers up to 4 inches wide. They are valued for their bright colors; names such as Crimson Star and Rose Queen indicate choices.

HOW TO GROW. Columbines are hardy in Zones 3-9 and grow best in a well-drained sandy soil. In rich, moist soil they will produce foliage but few flowers and will soon die. Plant columbines in early spring, as soon as the soil can be worked, or in the fall, when the plants are dormant. Space them 10 to 15 inches apart, and do not attempt to move them once they are established. Columbines are difficult to transplant except when they are small because they develop very long roots. Mulch plants where winters are severe, with a covering of salt hay, straw or leaves. New plants may be started from fresh seeds, collected in the summer as soon as they ripen, or from seeds sown indoors five to six weeks before the last frost. Plants raised from seed will bloom the second year.

ARISAEMA

A. dracontium (green dragon, dragonroot); *A. triphyllum* (Jack-in-the-pulpit)

For climate zones and frost dates, see maps, pages 152-153.

APPLE SERVICEBERRY
Amelanchier grandiflora

AMERICAN COLUMBINE
Aquilegia canadensis

JACK-IN-THE-PULPIT
Arisaema triphyllum

DUTCHMAN'S PIPE
Aristolochia durior

Long cherished for their curious blooms, these hardy long-lived perennials grow in any degree of shade from deep to open. They are most at home in naturalized settings and are especially pleasing when grouped with ferns.

Jack-in-the-pulpit, the better-known species, is named for its unusual green flower, a 3-inch-long finger-like spadix called the Jack standing erect within the arching, hooded pulpit, a leaflike spathe sometimes striped with red, purple, brown or white. The actual flowers cluster inconspicuously around the base of the Jack. The leaves, 4 to 6 inches long, spring in groups of three from a tall stem, stand 1 to 3 feet high and shade the blooms like an umbrella. In late summer or fall the flowers ripen into packed clusters of bright red berries, each up to ½ inch in diameter.

Green dragon grows up to 3 feet high, with a thin, twisting spadix that extends 5 or 6 inches above the unarched 3-inch spathe and is covered with greenish-yellow flowers. The leaves are 5 to 6 inches long and are composed of 5 to 15 leaflets growing at the top of each stem. Orange berries cover the spadix in late summer or fall.

HOW TO GROW. Both Jack-in-the-pulpit and green dragon are hardy in Zones 5-8 and grow best in moist, humus-rich acid soil. Jack-in-the-pulpit may be stunted if the soil remains dry; green dragon, however, tolerates a slightly dry soil. Sow seeds thinly in the fall, ¼ to ½ inch deep; they will germinate readily if fresh, although the plants may not produce top growth or bloom until the second year. To speed up this process, refrigerate the seeds at 40° in moist sand for six to 12 weeks before planting. Young plants may be transplanted any time, though late summer or early fall is best. Plants may also be propagated by separating offsets from their tuberous roots in the fall or early spring. If left undisturbed, plants will reseed themselves.

ARISTOLOCHIA

A. durior (Dutchman's pipe)

The extremely hardy Dutchman's pipe will thrive in medium to open shade and under difficult growing conditions: not even the smoggy atmosphere of urban environments can hamper this vigorously twining perennial vine. It quickly ascends a vertical support to a height of 20 to 30 feet, producing glossy green heart-shaped leaves, up to 12 inches long, which overlap to form a dense deciduous shade that easily covers walls, trellises or porches. Purplish-brown tubular flowers 3 inches long and curved like the stems of pipes begin to bloom in the spring of its second season.

HOW TO GROW. Dutchman's pipe is hardy in Zones 4-8 and flourishes in any well-drained garden soil. Set plants in the ground in fall or early spring, spacing them 4 feet apart. Fertilize each spring by scattering compost around the base of the vine. Water during dry spells. Young plants require a 4-inch mulch of dry leaves or coarse peat moss for winter protection their first year. Train Dutchman's pipe up a wire fence, trellis or vertical wires 1 foot apart, tying the stems to their support at intervals. In early spring remove weak branches and cut back one third. As new growth appears, pinch it back once or twice to encourage branching. Propagate Dutchman's pipe from stem cuttings taken in midsummer and rooted in a mixture of peat moss and sand or in the spring by fastening a stem to the ground until it takes root.

ARONIA

A. arbutifolia (red chokeberry); *A. melanocarpa* (black chokeberry)

For covering and brightening areas of low, damp ground in open shade, the native American chokeberry shrubs are an excellent choice. The shoots, or suckers, from the roots of a single plant may form colonies that cover an area larger than 12 feet square. Chokeberries flower in spring, their pink or white blossoms growing in clusters 2 inches across. In the autumn, their finely serrated leaves change color and their branches are decorated with summer-ripening berries that may linger on the plant through the winter. Red chokeberry is one of the few deciduous shrubs that will actually thrive in deep shade, though its fall color is better in lighter shade; black chokeberry needs the occasional sunlight of intermittent shade to promote the production of berries and autumn foliage color.

The red chokeberry grows from 6 to 9 feet high, fanning out from many stems. The leaves are smooth and oval, 1 to 3½ inches long; the white flowers are less than ½ inch wide and are borne in loose clusters of up to 20 blossoms that last for two or three weeks. Red berries, about ¼ inch in diameter, augment the scarlet of the autumn foliage. The variety *A. arbutifolia brilliantissima* has more and brighter fruits and leaves than the species.

Black chokeberry is smaller and more compact; it grows from 1½ to 3 feet high. The foliage is like that of the red chokeberry, but it turns purple in autumn. The flowers are white, and the berries are purple or purple-black.

HOW TO GROW. Chokeberries are hardy in Zones 4-8, growing best in moist soils, although the black chokeberry also adapts to dry soil. Plant in the spring, in holes about 6 inches wider than the root spread; fill the holes with a mixture of 2 parts topsoil to 1 part peat moss. Chokeberries are relatively pest free and rarely need pruning except to encourage branching. Propagate from suckers divided from the plant or from cuttings of new wood taken in spring.

ARROWWOOD See *Viburnum*

ASARUM

A. canadense (Canada wild ginger); *A. caudatum* (British Columbia wild ginger); *A. europaeum* (European wild ginger)

The wild gingers make excellent ground covers for medium to deep shade, the evergreen European and British Columbia wild gingers being more desirable for this purpose than the deciduous Canada wild ginger, which dies down in winter. All three species do well in the same soil conditions as mountain laurel and rhododendron and are often used with them. The wild gingers spread fairly rapidly by means of creeping underground stems, or rhizomes. They get their name from the ginger scent and flavor of the rhizomes, which are sometimes used as a seasoning, but the crushed leaves are also aromatic and the carpet itself has a spicy smell.

Canada wild ginger is 4 to 6 inches high, with soft, hairy, heart-shaped leaves 3 to 7 inches wide. Each stem bears a pair of branching leaves, which may emerge brown or red in the spring, before turning bronze-green; at the branch blooms a single brown flower, 1 inch wide, cup-shaped, with three lobes that end in ½-inch-long tails. Sometimes the flowers appear before the leaves have fully uncurled, but usually they are hidden at ground level by the foliage. The leaves of Canada wild ginger may irritate the skin.

British Columbia wild ginger grows 6 to 10 inches high, with shiny heart-shaped leaves, 2 to 6 inches long, that are sometimes tinged with bronze. Its flowers appear in spring but they too are usually hidden by the leaves; they are brown or red-purple, cup-shaped, and are ¾ inch wide with 2-inch-long tails. European wild ginger is 5 inches tall, with glossy kidney-shaped leaves 2 to 3 inches across. The brown or greenish-purple flowers appear in the spring and are

BRILLIANT CHOKEBERRY
Aronia arbutifolia brilliantissima

CANADA WILD GINGER
Asarum canadense

For climate zones and frost dates, see maps, pages 152-153.

MOTHER FERN
Asplenium bulbiferum

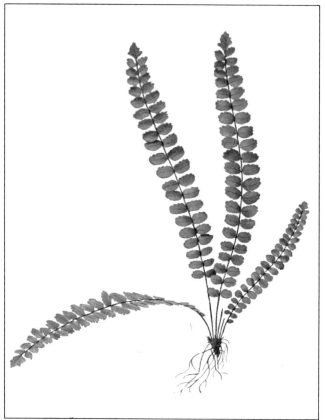

MAIDENHAIR SPLEENWORT
Asplenium trichomanes

about ½ inch wide. The flowers of all three species of wild ginger, though inconspicuous, last for many weeks before the large, thick seeds ripen.

HOW TO GROW. Wild gingers are hardy in Zones 4-10 and grow best in moist, slightly acid, humus-rich soil. Plant rhizomes in spring or fall, burying them ½ inch deep with just their tips showing above the soil level; space them 12 inches apart. Mulch new plants with oak or beech leaves or hay during the first winter to prevent the ground from heaving, and do not remove this cover in the spring. Propagate by division or from root cuttings taken in the summer and started in sand for autumn planting. Though collecting ripe seeds is difficult, wild gingers seed themselves freely.

ASPLENIUM
A. bulbiferum (mother fern, mother spleenwort); *A. trichomanes* (maidenhair spleenwort)

The spleenworts grow best when they are provided with deep shade and abundant moisture, although the hardy evergreen maidenhair spleenwort will flourish in medium shade as well, and it will even tolerate intermittent shade if it is frequently watered.

The deciduous mother fern eventually reaches a height of 2 feet. The dark, wiry central stalk is erect, marked with a double groove along its length and covered with scales; in two years it will be about 8 inches high. The 12- to 24-inch fronds appear in spring, spear shaped and 9 inches wide. The mother fern is of interest for two reasons. First, its foliage is of two distinct types: the leaflets of sterile fronds are delicate, sharply cut and feathery, while the somewhat narrower fertile fronds have rounded edges. Second, the mother fern bears numerous tiny bulblets, which appear on the upper surface of the fronds. The weight of these bulblets causes the fronds to bow gracefully toward the ground, where the bulblets take root, forming new ferns. The plant also reproduces itself from spore clusters that almost entirely cover one edge of the fertile fronds. Mother fern also spreads slowly by means of an underground stem, or rhizome.

Maidenhair spleenwort also grows from a rhizome, and eventually spreads to form a tuft of up to 250 fronds. The first fronds to appear in spring are sterile, the leaflets growing from a shiny black scale-covered stem nearly parallel to the ground. In summer the fertile fronds appear, erect in growth and 5 to 6 inches high. The sterile fronds are evergreen, but the fertile fronds will gradually fall off from late fall through early spring.

HOW TO GROW. Mother fern is hardy in Zones 9 and 10; maidenhair spleenwort is hardy in Zones 4-8. Mother fern does best in a neutral to slightly acid soil composed of 1 part garden loam, 1 part coarse sand and 2 parts leaf mold or peat moss. Maidenhair spleenwort prefers a neutral to slightly alkaline soil but will grow in moderately acid soil if well shaded. Add 2 tablespoons of ground limestone per cubic foot of the basic soil mixture. The soil for both ferns should be moist but well drained at all times. A mulch of leaves or evergreen boughs will help retain moisture while protecting the less-hardy roots of the mother fern during winter.

Plant spleenworts in spring, setting the mother fern 1 inch deep and 1 to 2 feet apart, the maidenhair spleenwort the same depth and 6 to 8 inches apart. Fertilize each spring by spreading bone meal around the base of the fern in the proportion of 1 ounce per square yard; or use fish emulsion fertilizer diluted to one half the strength recommended on the label. Dead fronds may be removed any time during the growing season. Spleenworts can be propagated from spores collected in midsummer or by root division. The easiest way to propagate mother fern is by transplanting the miniature ferns that grow from the bulblets in spring and summer. Place those on moist potting soil until they have rooted.

ASTILBE

A. arendsii hybrids (astilbe, false spirea)

Prized for both foliage and flowers, perennial astilbes grow well in both open and dappled shade and even tolerate deep shade. The plants grow best under deep-rooted trees such as ash, oak, sweet gum and honey locust. Although astilbes will grow in sun, shade intensifies the color of the flowers and makes them last longer. The lustrous, finely divided leaves have a fernlike appearance. Mounds of green-to-bronze foliage become 12 to 18 inches tall. In midsummer, feathery plumes of flowers are produced. Each 8- to 12-inch plume has a stalk 2 to 3 feet tall. Blooms last for several months. Of the *A. arendsii* hybrids, Peach Blossom is light pink, Rosy Veil is dark pink, and Red Sentinel is rich, bright red. A white variety is also available. Astilbes can be used in flower borders, massed as a ground cover, or planted with spring bulbs to hide their fading foliage. They produce excellent cut flowers and can be dried for winter arrangements.

HOW TO GROW. Astilbes can be grown throughout Zones 4-9. They do best in moist soil that has been enriched with organic matter such as peat moss, leaf mold or compost. The soil must be moist in summer but well drained in winter. Water frequently if the soil is light and sandy. Astilbes should be fertilized each spring with a high-phosphorus formula such as 5-10-5. Plants multiply rapidly, exhausting the soil around them; as they become overcrowded, they produce few flowers. To rejuvenate them, divide clumps in the spring or fall after two or three years of flowering. When you do so, work organic matter and a dusting of 0-20-20 fertilizer into the soil before replanting. Set plants 15 to 18 inches apart. Astilbes are relatively pest free.

ATHYRIUM

A. filix-femina (lady fern); *A. goeringianum pictum* (Japanese painted fern); *A. thelypteroides,* also called *Diplazium acrostichoides* (silvery glade fern)

The perennial athyriums are deciduous woodland ferns, 2 to 3 feet tall, that thrive in all degrees of shade, deep to open. Lady fern is the largest of the three. Its lance-shaped fronds grow 3 feet long and 15 inches wide, tapering at both ends. The fine-toothed leaflets are yellow-green when young, darker green as they mature, and are more closely crowded toward the end of their stem. New fronds continue to unfurl through the summer. Many varieties of lady fern are available, differing in shape and color, but all bear long, curved spore clusters along the central rib of each leaflet.

The Japanese painted fern is a colorful species with gray-green foliage and wine-red stems. It is 2 feet high, the fronds occupying only the top half of the stem. These fronds are spear shaped, tapering gracefully to a point from a width of 8 inches; the leaflets have a similar shape. A gray strip runs down the center of each leaflet and light-green spore clusters form in a herringbone pattern along the leaflet's central rib; the spores turn brown as they mature.

The silvery glade fern closely resembles the lady fern. However, its 3-foot lance-shaped fronds are about half as wide—7 inches—and its silvery spore clusters form herringbone patterns along the veins of the leaflets, imparting an overall sheen to the back of the fronds; as they mature, the spores turn blue-gray. The silvery glade fern has two types of foliage: sterile fronds, arching in habit, appear in spring at the perimeter of the plant; in summer, fertile fronds rise up

ASTILBE
Astilbe arendsii 'Rosy Veil'

JAPANESE PAINTED FERN
Athyrium goeringianum pictum

For climate zones and frost dates, see maps, pages 152-153.

WAX BEGONIA
Begonia semperflorens

TOP: HARDY BEGONIA, *Begonia grandis*
BOTTOM: TUBEROUS BEGONIA, *B. tuberhybrida* 'Double Ruffled Apricot'

in the plant's center, more erect, more slender and taller. The leaflets of both types are yellow-green when young, then deep green and finally reddish brown in late summer. The leaflet segments may be either smooth or serrated along their edges. New ones develop through late summer.

All three of these ferns spread slowly by means of underground stems, or rhizomes, to form colonies. They are useful in foundation plantings against building walls, and to fill in the spaces between taller plants or shrubs.

HOW TO GROW. Athyriums are hardy in Zones 3-8, and do best in an acid soil composed of 1 part garden loam, 1 part coarse sand and 2 parts leaf mold or peat moss. The soil should be moist but well drained at all times. A mulch of leaves or evergreen boughs will help retain moisture while protecting the roots during winter.

Plant athyriums in the spring or fall, setting them 1 inch deep and 1½ to 2 feet apart. Fertilize each spring, spreading bone meal around the base of the fern in the proportion of 1 ounce per square yard; or use fish emulsion diluted to half the strength recommended. Remove dead fronds in early spring before new growth appears. Propagate from spores collected in mid- or late summer, or by root division.

AZALEA See *Rhododendron*

B

BABY-BLUE-EYES See *Nemophila*
BALSAM, GARDEN See *Impatiens*
BEAD FERN See *Onoclea*

BEGONIA

B. grandis, also called *B. evansiana* (hardy begonia, Evans begonia); *B. semperflorens* (wax begonia); *B. tuberhybrida* (tuberous begonia)

Besides bearing mounds of foliage—green, bronze or variegated—begonias bloom in open or intermittent shade, flowering through the summer and up to the first frost. They can be used as bedding or border plants under high-branching trees, in window boxes on north-facing walls or in baskets hung where the slanting rays of the sun can reach them early or late in the day. They will not flourish in deep shade.

The hardy begonia dies to the ground in winter but survives cold in Zone 8 and is hardy farther north if given protection. It grows from tuberous roots, its branching succulent stems reaching 2 to 3 feet in height. Small pink flowers bloom in drooping clusters above the leaves, which are 3 to 6 inches long and are green with red veins on the upper surfaces, red underneath. The tiny bulblike tubers that appear at the leaf joints in spring can be used for propagating.

The wax begonias are fibrous-rooted low-growing bushy plants, 6 to 9 inches tall or taller, depending on the variety. They grow in Zones 6-10 and may bloom almost continuously year round in Zones 9 and 10. North of Zone 6, wax begonias may be grown outdoors in summer and moved indoors before the first frost. Their succulent branching stems are covered with shiny heart-shaped leaves, 2 to 4 inches long, of green, bronze-red or mahogany. Close-clustered white, pink, rose or red flowers sometimes cover the little bush entirely. Among the varieties that bloom most profusely in shade are Butterfly, with large white, pink, red or deep rose flowers; Calla Queen, with scarlet flowers and green and white variegated leaves; Linda Bright, with small pink blooms, and the ivory double-flowered White Christmas.

Tuberous hybrid begonias grow in Zones 3-10 but must be dug up and replanted each year because they will not survive winter cold. Many gardeners find it simpler to use them as pot plants, moving the pots indoors each fall. Tuberous hybrid begonias (such as the Double Ruffled Apricot variety) outflower other species in both number and size of blooms and range of color. Their flowers are 2 to 10 inches wide and appear singly, in pairs or in threes in white or shades of yellow, orange, rose, red and pink. Equally versatile in its growth habit, the tuberous hybrid begonia comes in upright varieties 12 to 18 inches tall, in short, bushy varieties up to 10 inches tall or with trailing stems 12 to 18 inches long. Any of these varieties are good for shady locations.

HOW TO GROW. All begonias grow best in a moist but well-drained 6-inch-deep mixture consisting of 2 parts loam and 2 parts peat moss to 1 part builder's sand. All three species should be started indoors and not set out until night temperatures have risen to 50°.

Start hardy and tuberous begonias about two months before planting time. Place the tubers, hollow side up, in damp, well-drained peat moss. When the roots are established and shoots are about 1 or 2 inches high, move them to pots 4 to 6 inches wide filled with the same soil the plants will grow in when they are set outdoors. Give them strong light from east, south or west windows and turn them occasionally to make sure their formation is symmetrical. Keep the soil moist. When all danger of frost has passed, move them outdoors.

Set hardy begonias in the garden about 6 inches apart with the crowns 1 or 2 inches below ground level; mulch them in winter. Set large-flowered tuberous begonias in the garden 12 to 15 inches apart, staking upright varieties with wire or bamboo; take care not to pierce the tubers. Dig up tubers in the fall before frost and put them in flats. Let the plants ripen in a sunny, airy place. When leaves and stems die, clean and store the tubers indoors in peat moss at a temperature of 40° to 50°.

Sow seeds for wax begonias four to six months before planting time; set plants 6 to 8 inches apart in the garden. Plants may also be started indoors from stem cuttings taken in the spring or fall or by division in the fall; the latter method results in better-branching, stronger plants.

BERGENIA
B. crassifolia (leather bergenia, Siberian tea leaves)

Leather bergenia, a perennial with fleshy cabbage-like leaves 8 or more inches wide, grows best in open shade. From thick underground stems, the plants form clumps 2 to 3 feet wide and 10 to 12 inches tall. Flower stalks up to 18 inches tall appear in early spring, bearing clusters of ¾-inch pink to reddish-purple bell-shaped blooms. The foliage is evergreen in Zones 7-10 but turns bronze in the fall in Zones 4-6. This bold foliage and the plants' bright flowers make them useful as accents along shady pathways or rocky banks of streams. One variety, *B. crassifolia aureo-marginata,* has multicolored foliage.

HOW TO GROW. Leather bergenia is hardy in Zones 4-10. It tolerates almost any soil but does best in moist, rich, acid soil. Start plants in spring, setting them 12 to 15 inches apart. Pinch off flower stems after the blooms fade. Propagate by dividing plants immediately after they have finished flowering. Leather bergenia may also be grown from seed, but it takes two years to become established.

BISHOP'S HAT See *Epimedium*
BLEEDING HEART See *Dicentra*
BLUEBELL See *Mertensia*
BLUETS See *Houstonia*
BOULDER FERN See *Dennstaedtia*
BRAKEROOT See *Polypodium*

LEATHER BERGENIA
Bergenia crassifolia

For climate zones and frost dates, see maps, pages 152-153.

BLUE TROLL BROWALLIA
Browallia speciosa major 'Blue Troll'

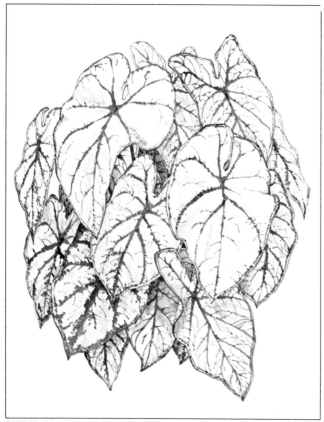

CANDIDUM FANCY-LEAVED CALADIUM
Caladium hortulanum 'Candidum'

BROWALLIA
B. speciosa major 'Blue Troll' (bush violet)

An easily grown annual for open shade, browallia blooms all summer long, its velvety flowers, 1 inch across, rising above the glossy, bright green foliage. It comes in several forms: as compact bushes 6 to 10 inches tall with many-branching stems, as upright-growing varieties 36 inches tall, or with graceful trailing stems that rise to a height of 14 to 16 inches and spread the same distance. The flowers are shades of blue and lavender, as well as pure white. Compact varieties such as Blue Troll are excellent in pots, as an edging or massed in beds; the spreading types are useful in tubs, in hanging baskets or along rock walls where they can cascade over the edges.

HOW TO GROW. Browallias grow in Zones 3-10 and do best in a moderately rich, well-drained but evenly moist soil. Mulch them to maintain moisture, and feed them monthly with a general-purpose fertilizer.

BUGBANE See *Cimicifuga*
BUGLEWEED See *Ajuga*
BUNCHBERRY See *Cornus*
BUSH VIOLET See *Browallia*

C
CALADIUM
C. hortulanum (fancy-leaved caladium)

The beautifully marked foliage of fancy-leaved caladiums shows up most dramatically in the open shade of a covered terrace or walled garden, or in the filtered light provided by deciduous trees. They will tolerate a small amount of weak early morning or late afternoon sun but must be protected from the hot midday light. The thin translucent leaves also need shelter from wind or they will fray and tatter. But they do withstand city smoke and dirt. The leaves are heart-shaped, with straight or wavy edges, and range in size from 6 to 24 inches long. Their markings may be red, white, salmon, silver or pink, and one variety, Candidum, has white leaves with dark green markings. The foliage quite overshadows the occasional pale pink flower spikes that appear on 6-inch stalks in early summer. The plant grows about 1 foot tall.

HOW TO GROW. Although caladiums need four full months of active growth to store food in the tuber for the following year, they cannot remain outdoors year round except in Zone 10. In Zones 3-9 start them indoors six to eight weeks before outdoor temperatures during the day average about 70°. Pot them in a mixture of equal parts of coarse sand, loam and peat moss or ground bark, with a half teaspoonful of 5-10-5 fertilizer added for each 4-inch potful of the mix. Place each tuber in the pot with its knobby side up and cover it with 1 to 2 inches of soil.

Keep the soil barely damp and the surrounding air between 70° and 85° until the plant's growth is active; then keep the soil constantly moist. Outdoors, set caladiums 12 inches apart and water weekly if there is little rain. Dust the soil around the plants with a general-purpose balanced fertilizer every two to three weeks during the growing season.

In fall, gradually withhold water until all the leaves die down; then remove the tubers carefully from the earth, lay them in a dry, semishaded place for about 10 days and, finally, brush off the dirt. Sprinkle them with an insecticide-fungicide preparation and store them at 55° to 60° in dry peat moss or vermiculite. To propagate, divide the tubers, leaving two to three buds on each section to get a plant with multiple stems. Dust exposed surfaces with fungicide and let the tubers dry for two days before replanting.

CALICO BUSH See *Kalmia*

CALYCANTHUS
C. floridus (sweet shrub, Carolina allspice, strawberry shrub)

Prized for its aromatic leaves, bark and flowers, the sweet shrub flourishes in both open and medium shade. It is a deciduous plant that usually grows 5 to 6 feet tall, spreading equally wide, but it may reach heights of 10 feet. The dark green leathery leaves, 2 to 5 inches long, have fuzzy brown undersides; they turn yellow in the fall. This foliage, when crushed or rubbed, has a spicy fragrance. In late spring a profusion of 2-inch brownish-red flowers fills the air with perfume that smells at first like strawberries but changes to the aroma of ripe apples. The flowers have many ribbon-like petals and sepals that are similar in size, shape and color.

HOW TO GROW. Sweet shrub grows in Zones 5-10 in any moderately rich soil that is moist and well drained. Add 1 part of peat moss or leaf mold for every 2 parts of soil if it is necessary to enrich it or improve drainage. Select a position protected from the wind and keep the ground evenly cool and moist; if necessary use a permanent mulch of wood chips, ground bark or chunky peat moss 3 to 4 inches deep. Sweet shrub normally should not be fertilized because feeding encourages growth of foliage rather than flowers, but a weak plant may be strengthened with a light scattering of cottonseed meal around the plant in early spring.

Prune in early spring before growth begins. Start new plants from cuttings of new growth. New plants may also be started from arching stems that have taken root or from suckers growing from rooted underground stems.

CAMELLIA
C. japonica (common camellia); *C. sasanqua* (sasanqua camellia)

An evergreen shrub with shiny leaves and spectacular red, white, pink or multicolored flowers, the camellia is at its best in the gentle light of open shade. It needs protection from hot midday sun, but deep shade inhibits flowering. So does hot, dry weather, which sometimes causes unopened buds to drop off. Camellia flowers generally grow in clusters and the most popular forms have multiple layers of petals.

The tender common camellia usually grows 6 to 10 feet tall in 10 to 15 years, although in southern gardens it may reach a height of 30 feet. It has wide leaves 2½ to 4 inches long, and waxy flowers 2 to 9 inches wide. Flowering begins in midfall on early-blooming varieties, reaches a peak in early spring and continues into midspring on later-blooming kinds. Among the best early-flowering multipetaled types are Alba Plena with white flowers and Daikagura with rose-red flowers mottled with white. Three later-blooming multipetaled varieties that grow well in the northern parts of the camellia's range are Betty Sheffield Supreme with pink-edged white flowers, Chandleri Elegans with white-splashed rose flowers and Kramer's Supreme with dark red flowers.

Sasanqua camellia, an autumn-blooming species, becomes 5 or 6 feet tall in about 10 years and may ultimately reach 20 feet. It has narrow 2-inch-long leaves and blooms from early fall to early winter. Three recommended multipetaled varieties are Cleopatra with pink flowers, Sparkling Burgundy with dark pink to red flowers and White Doves (also called Mine-No-Yuk) with white flowers.

Both common and sasanqua camellias are widely grown as informal hedges and they are often used to screen unsightly walls and foundations; they also make good accent plants.

HOW TO GROW. Common and sasanqua camellias grow best in Zones 8-10. Although the plants tolerate some sun along

SWEET SHRUB
Calycanthus floridus

COMMON CAMELLIA
Camellia japonica

For climate zones and frost dates, see maps, pages 152-153.

EASTERN REDBUD
Cercis canadensis

FRINGE TREE
Chionanthus virginicus

the Gulf Coast, where the air and soil are constantly moist, in more northern areas they must be protected from sun until the plants become well established, to prevent their roots from drying out. Both species grow best in locations sheltered from winter winds and the sasanqua camellia is sometimes damaged by heavy rains. Plant in acid soil; a mixture of 1 part peat moss to 1 part sandy loam is best. Keep the ground evenly moist, never soggy and never dry. In zones where there is some danger of the ground's freezing, provide a permanent mulch of wood chips, ground bark or chunky peat moss 3 to 4 inches deep.

In Zones 9 and 10 set out balled-and-burlaped plants from fall to spring; in Zone 8, set out in spring. Place plants so the original soil line, visible at the base of the stems, is 1 inch above the new soil level; camellia roots must not be smothered. In very hot weather, hose down the leaves to keep them moist and to wash off insects. To encourage good stem growth, fertilize every eight weeks from spring until early fall with cottonseed meal or a special rhododendron-azalea-camellia fertilizer, scratching it lightly into the soil around the plants. Reduce feeding if it appears that excessive vegetative growth is being made at the expense of flower production. Prune only in the spring, during and just after flowering. Propagate by rooting stem cuttings in midsummer.

CARDINAL FLOWER See *Lobelia*
CAROLINA ALLSPICE See *Calycanthus*

CERCIS

C. canadensis (eastern redbud, American redbud, Judas tree)

Eastern redbud, a profusely flowering small tree, does well in open shade, but it needs some sun in late winter and spring to stimulate the most lavish display of flowers. It normally grows 10 to 15 feet tall and may eventually reach a height of up to 35 feet. The eastern redbud's ½-inch pink-purple flowers open in early spring, before the leaves unfurl, and are followed by 2- to 4-inch greenish seed pods that ripen to brown and remain on the branches well into the following winter. The shiny green heart-shaped leaves, 3 to 5 inches wide, open in late spring, changing to yellow in fall before dropping off. One variety, *C. canadensis alba,* bears white flowers. Eastern redbud is a useful accent tree for any shaded location, and is often planted next to dogwood, which flowers about the same time. However, redbud does not bloom until the tree is four or five years old, and leaves are slow to develop the first season after planting.

HOW TO GROW. Eastern redbud is hardy in Zones 5-10 and thrives in a moist, well-drained, deeply cultivated soil. Buy young trees less than 6 feet tall with their roots balled and burlaped in the original soil. In Zones 5-7, set out trees in spring; in Zones 8-10, plant at any time from fall to spring. Normally trees do not require fertilizing, but a weak tree may be strengthened by applying a dusting of cottonseed meal or an all-purpose fertilizer in spring.

CHECKERBERRY See *Gaultheria*

CHIONANTHUS

C. virginicus (fringe tree, old-man's beard)

The fringe tree is a small flowering tree that blooms well in open or intermittent shade, although it needs some sun in spring to produce abundant flowers. This slow-growing tree ranges in height from 10 to 30 feet, spreading almost equally wide, and may have one or several trunks. The 3- to 8-inch-long leaves do not appear until late spring or even early summer, but as soon as they do, the branches are also decorated with fragrant flowers in dangling clusters, 6 to 8 inches long, that look like shredded paper; each silky flower has four petals an inch long and less than ¼ inch wide. Male trees bear larger clusters than female trees, but on the latter the blossoms are followed by grapelike clusters of dark blue egg-shaped fruits, each ½ to ¾ inch long, which contrast with the golden-yellow autumn foliage. A fringe tree is an effective accent tree near a house, but it should not be placed near a terrace or path where its falling blossoms and fruit might be messy.

HOW TO GROW. The fringe tree is hardy in Zones 5-10. It does best in a moist, well-drained soil cultivated deeply to accommodate its long roots. Choose a location with some protection from winter winds. Buy trees with their roots balled and burlaped in the original soil, setting them out in spring in Zones 5-7 and at any time from fall to spring in Zones 8-10. Established trees normally do not need to be fertilized, but a weak tree may be strengthened by sprinkling cottonseed meal or an all-purpose fertilizer around its base in spring. They do not require pruning to maintain their shape but may be pruned if desired. Male trees should be pruned after their flowers fade in summer, female trees in early winter, after their fruits are gone.

CHOKEBERRY See *Aronia*

CIMICIFUGA
C. racemosa (cohosh bugbane, black cohosh, black snakeroot, fairy candles); *C. simplex,* also called *C. foetida intermedia* (Kamchatka bugbane)

The towering bugbanes, which take their common name from an insect-repellent scent, grow in deep to open shade and rank among the most impressive woodland wildflowers. They grow up to 8 feet tall, produce leaves up to 2 feet long, and bear spires of tiny white flowers up to 4 feet high. The latter earn them the common name of fairy candles. Their height and coarse foliage make bugbanes excellent background plants in the shade garden.

Cohosh bugbane ranges from 5 to 8 feet in height and blooms in mid- to late summer. The flower spike is commonly 2 feet tall but may reach 4 feet. The compound leaves are made up of 2- to 4-inch thin, tapering leaflets, toothed or deeply cut. One variety, *C. racemosa cordifolia,* has heart-shaped leaflets. The smaller Kamchatka bugbane grows 2 to 4 feet tall and blooms in fall. The flower spike may be 3 feet long. The more compact variety White Pearl is noted for its pure white flowers, whiter than those of other bugbanes.

HOW TO GROW. Bugbanes are hardy in Zones 4-9 in moist, acid soil enriched with peat moss or leaf mold. Plant rootstock in the spring or fall, setting the roots 1 to 1½ inches deep and 12 inches apart, or set out nursery-grown seedlings in early spring or fall. Bugbane may also be started from seeds collected and planted in the fall as soon as they ripen. Bugbanes have deep roots; water thoroughly during dry weather. Mulch in fall with 2 inches of compost. Additional plants may be propagated by dividing established clumps in the spring, but it is best to leave bugbane undisturbed.

CLEMATIS
C. hybrids (all called clematis, virgin's bower)

The twining clematis vine, a perennial, flourishes in open shade; its roots need to be cool and moist. However, its foliage and flowers require some sunshine. To meet these dual needs, plant clematis where the roots will be shaded by a low wall or a building, low shrubs or a ground cover. Although clematis will tolerate the light conditions of a north-

KAMCHATKA BUGBANE
Cimicifuga simplex 'White Pearl'

For climate zones and frost dates, see maps, pages 152-153.

ern exposure, it will seek the sun and tend to produce most of its flowers near the ends of stems, acceptable in some situations but not in others. Clematis quickly reaches its maximum height of 12 feet in a single season, twisting its leaf stems around a thin support. Its deciduous heart-shaped leaves, 3 to 5 inches long, will cover a wall, fence, trellis, arch, pillar, post or porch, but it is the large flowers—in bloom from summer to fall—that earn clematis vines their great popularity. Actually these flowers are made up of sepals; petals are nonexistent. In the fall the flowers are followed by seeds with long silvery plumes.

Jackman clematis produces purple flowers, 5 or 6 inches wide, with four to six sepals; they bloom either singly or in clusters of two or three on new growth and have green stamens at their centers. The hybrids Henryi and Ramona produce flowers on both old and new growth and therefore begin to bloom earlier. The 6- to 8-inch flowers of Henryi have six to eight creamy white sepals and dark brown stamens; the 5- or 6-inch flowers of Ramona are lavender with deep blue stamens. Because it is susceptible to cedar rust, clematis should not be planted near evergreens that are likely to suffer the disease.

HOW TO GROW. Clematis are hardy in Zones 5-8. They need a rich, well-drained loamy soil, neutral to slightly alkaline. As young plants are tender and may fail, it is best to purchase established clematis stock, at least two years old. Plant clematis vines 6 feet apart in holes 3 feet deep and 2 feet wide; place 2 inches of rock or gravel on the bottom for drainage. Set the plants in the holes so their root tops are 2 inches below the surface of the soil, and fill the holes with equal parts of soil, compost and sand. Support young vines with stakes and guard them against mechanical injury with collars made of sheet metal. Pinch out new shoots once or twice to encourage branching. Train the vine to a thin vertical support, tying the stems to the support at intervals. Water generously and mulch with 4 inches of leaf mold to preserve moisture; in its first year clematis must never be allowed to become dry. Thereafter water during dry spells.

Fertilize clematis each spring and fall by scattering an all-purpose fertilizer around the base of the vine, and after the first year, feed every 10 days during its period of bloom. If soil is naturally acid, add lime every year or two. Henryi and Ramona should not be pruned except to remove dead or weak stems, but Jackman should be pruned after it is well established; in about two years, prune it at the end of winter, cutting the vine back to within 9 inches of the ground, leaving only one pair of buds. Propagate from stem cuttings taken in early summer and rooted in a mixture of peat moss and sand. Or start new plants by fastening a section of stem against the ground until it takes root; clematis roots most successfully from a point between nodes.

CINNAMON FERN See *Osmunda*

CLETHRA
C. alnifolia 'Rosea' (pink summer sweet, sweet pepper bush); *C. barbinervis* (Japanese clethra)

A deciduous shrub native to woodlands, the clethra grows well in the dappled light and open shade of tall deciduous trees. It tolerates wind and salty sea air, and will thrive in wet soil, making the plant especially useful for coastal locations. The plant is notable because it produces sweetly scented flowers in dense spikes 3 to 5 inches long in late summer; the flowers last four to six weeks and are excellent for cutting. They are followed by dangling seed pods which many gardeners prefer to remove for a neater appearance.

CLEMATIS
Clematis jackmanii

Pink summer sweet grows 4 to 6 feet tall and bears pink-tinged flowers; its shiny leaves, 1½ to 4 inches long, turn yellow in the fall and form foliage so thick that the plant is sometimes sheared as a hedge. Japanese clethra, a less hardy species, ranges from 10 to 30 feet in height; its white flower spikes are 4 to 6 inches long and grow horizontally from the branches. Both species, which spread by underground stems, are useful as background plants for a border or as single accent plants for color in the shade. In dry weather, clethra may be attacked by red spider mites; of the two species, Japanese clethra tends to be less susceptible to the insects.

HOW TO GROW. Pink summer sweet grows well in Zones 4-9; Japanese clethra is hardy in Zones 7-10. Both thrive in moist acid soil enriched with generous amounts of peat moss or leaf mold. If necessary, keep the soil moist with a permanent mulch of wood chips, ground bark or chunky peat moss 3 to 4 inches deep. Normally clethra does not need to be fertilized, but a weak plant may be strengthened by lightly scattering cottonseed meal around its base in early spring.

Clip off faded flowers to stimulate new growth and to prevent seed pods from forming. Prune overly long branches in the early spring while the plant is still dormant; the new growth that results will produce flowers by summer. Propagate additional plants from cuttings of new wood taken in the late spring or early summer, or from hardened stems in mid- or late fall. New plants may also be started by cutting off and replanting suckers from the underground stems.

CLIMBING BIRD'S NEST FERN See *Polypodium*
COHOSH, BLACK See *Cimicifuga*
COHOSH BUGBANE See *Cimicifuga*

COLEUS
C. hybrids (coleus)

Sites with open or intermittent shade are ideal for coleus because the soft light intensifies the rich colors of the foliage. Due to extensive breeding, many strains of coleus are available. All of them form spreading mounds, but they differ in size, color and configuration of leaf. They may range in height from 6 inches to 2 feet, and their leaves may be oval or very narrow and have toothed edges, deep lobes, serrations or ruffles. Their many possible colors include yellow, chartreuse, green, white, cream, brown, red, crimson, salmon, pink, maroon, orange, bronze and purple, and these may appear in a wide assortment of combinations and patterns.

All are hybrids, tracing their parentage back to the 3- to 6-foot-tall *C. blumei,* to the 1½- to 3-foot-tall *C. pumilus* and to other species. *C. pumilus,* besides contributing shorter growth, accounts for the creeping stem, deeply toothed leaves and three-colored patterns found in many coleuses. Typical of the varieties is Rose Wizard, which grows 10 inches tall and has leaves up to 4 inches long, bright rose in the center, with cream and green edges. In their native habitat, coleuses grow as perennials, but they are generally grown as annuals in cooler temperate-zone gardens. They are used in beds and borders as edging plants or in masses, as well as in pots, hanging containers and window boxes.

HOW TO GROW. Coleuses are winter-hardy only in Zone 10, but they can be cultivated as summer annuals almost anywhere and do well in a wide range of garden soils. They do best, however, if they are kept evenly moist and are fed monthly with an all-purpose fertilizer. Mulch if necessary to maintain soil moisture. Although most gardeners purchase nursery-grown seedlings or rooted cuttings, common coleus can be started from seeds sown indoors 10 weeks before the last frost is due. Do not cover the seeds. With bottom heat of

PINK SUMMER SWEET
Clethra alnifolia 'Rosea'

ROSE WIZARD COLEUS
Coleus hybrid 'Rose Wizard'

For climate zones and frost dates, see maps, pages 152-153.

LILY OF THE VALLEY
Convallaria majalis

BUNCHBERRY
Cornus canadensis

70°, seeds germinate in 10 days. Move plants into the garden when all frost danger is past, spacing them 8 to 10 inches apart. The first several pairs of leaves may not be variegated; colors will develop later and the most intense colors are usually found in vigorous seedlings. To encourage the best foliage display, pinch off the growing tips of newly planted coleus and remove the insignificant flower clusters as soon as they appear, later in the season. You can easily propagate additional coleuses of any variety from stem cuttings, rooting them in water or moist sand.

COLUMBINE See *Aquilega*
COMMON POLYPODY See *Polypodium*

CONVALLARIA

C. majalis (lily of the valley)

The delicate bell-shaped flowers of lily of the valley perfume woodland gardens in midspring, and the plant's foliage then forms a cool green ground cover or edging in the open shade of high-branching trees, vine-covered trellises or sheltered terraces. In dense shade a carpet of leaves will grow, but there will be few flowers. The plants spread rapidly by underground stems called pips. At maturity, the plant has two elliptical leaves, 8 inches long and 1 to 3 inches wide, and a wiry stalk containing five to eight white ¼-inch flowers. In autumn the plants die to the ground, but they re-emerge in spring for many years. They require little or no cultivation, are rarely invasive and tolerate urban smog.

HOW TO GROW. Lily of the valley is hardy in Zones 3-8. It grows most luxuriantly in the colder zones and does best in rich, damp, acid soil. Set out plants or pips in the fall or early spring, spacing them 5 inches apart and covering them with 1 inch of earth. Although they need little further care, they will continue to produce more flowers if covered with a thin layer of compost in the fall to keep them from being heaved out of the ground by frost. To propagate, dig up rhizomes in the fall after the plant's foliage yellows or in spring when leaves emerge, divide them into sections with at least one pip on each section, and replant.

CORNUS

C. canadensis (bunchberry, dwarf cornel, crackerberry); *C. florida* (flowering dogwood); *C. nuttallii* (mountain dogwood, Nuttall's dogwood, Pacific dogwood, western dogwood)

Ornamental in all seasons, the ever-popular dogwood trees grow to best advantage in open shade. Their low-growing relative, the bunchberry, flourishes in deep shade. The distinctive flowers of the *Cornus* genus are not truly flowers but petal-like bracts; the real flowers are tiny and nestle inside. In late summer and fall, both dogwood and bunchberry produce clusters of bright red fruit.

Bunchberry grows only 5 to 9 inches tall, spreading rapidly on creeping underground stems, or rhizomes. Its 3-inch-long leaves, arranged in circular whorls, die down to the ground in winter, reappearing the following spring. The flowers, less than 1 inch wide, are composed of four to six white petal-like bracts. These open in late spring or early summer, and are followed by clusters of ¼-inch berries. This fast-spreading plant is a useful ground cover under trees and shrubs, especially in woodland settings.

The flowering dogwood grows 15 to 30 feet tall with horizontal branches that spread 15 to 20 feet wide. Its white or pink flower-like bracts are 3 to 6 inches across and appear in midspring before the leaves unfurl. There are four bracts, each with a distinctive notch at the tip; these are succeeded in fall by ¼-inch red berries. The leaves are 3 to 4 inches long and have a pinkish hue when they unfurl, changing to green in summer and red in the fall. The sooty black bark develops deep grooves that give it a checkerboard pattern, most noticeable on older trees. Some recommended white-flowering varieties are White Cloud, Cherokee Princess, Gigantea and Magnifica; Pluribracteata, with double flowers; Welchii, with pink-splashed white flowers; and *C. florida pendula,* with drooping branches. Good pink varieties include Apple Blossom, Spring Song and Cherokee Chief.

The mountain dogwood grows 20 to 30 feet tall. Unlike other species, its 4- to 5-inch blooms have four to seven bracts; these are sometimes tinged with pink. The flowers appear in spring, and frequently again in fall, along with red-orange inch-wide fruit clusters that are made up of 30 or 40 minuscule berries. The 3- to 5-inch leaves turn yellow and red in fall. Both flowering and mountain dogwoods are effective under taller trees or as accent trees on the shady lawn.

HOW TO GROW. Bunchberry is hardy in Zones 2-7; flowering dogwood in Zones 5-9; mountain dogwood in Zones 7-9—but only on the West Coast. Bunchberry needs cold, acid boglike soil rich in sphagnum moss. Flowering and mountain dogwood do best in moist, well-drained acid soil supplemented with peat moss or leaf mold; they cannot tolerate either constantly wet soil or drought, the latter condition making them vulnerable to attack by dogwood borer.

Plant bunchberry in spring or fall in groups of two or three, spacing them about a foot apart. Keep the ground cool and moist by providing a mulch, 2 to 3 inches deep, of old leaves or pine needles. For dogwood trees, choose a location with some protection from cold winds, so that buds are not destroyed; pink-flowering types are especially susceptible to cold winds. In southern zones, trees must have open shade at all times, but in northern areas, the flowering dogwood can tolerate some sun—not, however, in the hottest part of the day. Buy trees under 10 feet tall with their roots balled and burlaped in the original soil.

Plant dogwoods in spring after the soil has warmed. Normally they do not need to be fertilized, and they should not be pruned because they are slow to heal. To keep lawn mowers from hitting the trunks, spread a mulch of wood chips or ground bark, 2 to 3 inches deep, around the tree to a diameter of 2 feet or more. Similarly, to protect young trunks from rodents, wrap them with 12-inch-wide coarse screening. Additional bunchberry plants may be propagated from seeds separated from their pulp as soon as the berries ripen. Sow them ¼ inch deep in a mixture of 3 parts sand to 1 part sphagnum moss and transplant the seedlings when they appear two or three years later.

CORYDALIS
C. lutea (yellow corydalis), *C. nobilis* (Siberian corydalis)

Growing best in open or intermittent shade, perennial corydalis also tolerates deep shade. The finely divided fern-like foliage remains attractive through the summer. Spikes of small flowers bloom from midspring to early summer. Corydalises are useful plants for borders, retaining walls or rock gardens. The flowers are often used in flower arrangements.

Yellow corydalis, a bushy plant with many stems, grows 12 to 15 inches tall. It is often called yellow bleeding heart. The ¾-inch yellow flowers are borne on spikes above the foliage and sometimes continue blooming until midsummer or later. Siberian corydalis is a more open plant with fewer stems. Velvety foliage grows up to 30 inches tall. The 1-inch cream-colored flowers have yellow and purple markings.

HOW TO GROW. Yellow corydalis grows in Zones 6-8 except along the Gulf Coast; Siberian corydalis grows in Zones 3-8.

For climate zones and frost dates, see maps, pages 152-153.

MOUNTAIN DOGWOOD
Cornus nuttallii

YELLOW CORYDALIS
Corydalis lutea

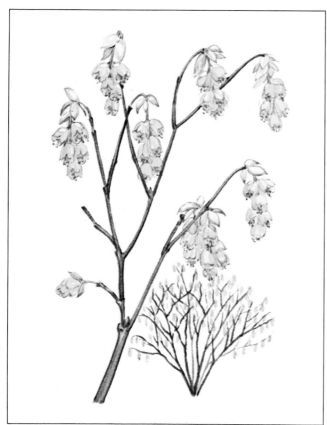

SPIKE WINTER HAZEL
Corylopsis spicata

SHOWY LADY'S SLIPPER
Cypripedium reginae

Both require soil with excellent drainage that will dry between waterings. Supplement the soil with organic matter such as peat moss or leaf mold. Apply an all-purpose fertilizer in the spring. Propagate from seeds or from stem cuttings taken in summer; plants started from cuttings will bloom the following summer. Divide plants in early spring after two or three years of flowering. Space yellow corydalis 8 to 10 inches apart, Siberian corydalis 12 to 18 inches apart.

CORYLOPSIS

C. pauciflora (buttercup winter hazel); *C. sinensis* (Chinese winter hazel); *C. spicata* (spike winter hazel)

Among the earliest shrubs to flower in spring, the winter hazels grow best in medium to open shade. They need some sunshine in early spring to stimulate flowering. Flower buds open long before the foliage appears, dangling in clusters of fragrant bell-shaped yellow flowers from bare branches. The 2-inch leaves that follow are deep green in summer, with dark parallel veins, and they often turn golden in the autumn. Winter hazel usually has a spread equal to its height and seldom requires pruning.

Buttercup winter hazel grows 3 to 5 feet tall and bears clusters of two or three small flowers, each ½ inch long. Chinese winter hazel usually remains under 6 feet tall, but may grow to 15 feet. Its downy leaves have a bluish cast in summer; the ¾-inch flowers form drooping 2-inch-long clusters. Spike winter hazel grows 4 to 6 feet tall and blooms more prolifically than the other two species, producing many ⅜-inch flowers in pendant clusters up to 3 inches long, but its leaves do not change color in fall; they wither and die.

Because of their early flowers and thick summer foliage, the winter hazels are especially useful planted against bare walls or as informal hedges.

HOW TO GROW. Winter hazels are hardy in Zones 6-9. They thrive in moist, acid soil well supplemented with peat moss or leaf mold. They should be given a sheltered location to protect them from winter winds, intense cold and sudden temperature drops; otherwise exposed buds may be killed. In areas where the ground freezes deeply, apply a permanent mulch of wood chips, ground bark or chunky peat moss 3 to 4 inches thick.

Normally, winter hazels do not need fertilizing. Pruning is seldom required except to remove old or weak branches. Propagate by taking stem cuttings of ripening new wood in spring, by division of the root clumps or by anchoring low-hanging branches to the ground until they take root.

CREEPING CHARLIE See *Lysimachia*
CREEPING JENNY See *Lysimachia*
CRESTED POLYPODY See *Polypodium*
CRIMSON GLORY VINE See *Vitis*

CYPRIPEDIUM

C. acaule (pink lady's slipper, pink moccasin flower), *C. reginae* (showy lady's slipper)

Lady's slipper orchids require shade to thrive, though it may range from open to deep. Their other requirements are more precise. In general, a perennial lady's slipper can be established only where wild colonies of that species are growing nearby, for each kind requires that there be a specific woodland fungus in the soil. Both of the species listed have a pouch-shaped lower petal that resembles a slipper or moccasin, and both bloom in summer.

Pink lady's slipper produces one 4-inch-wide flower atop each 8- to 20-inch stem. The pouch is usually pink with red veins, but there is also a white variety. Two 4- to 8-inch yellow-green leaves join the stem at ground level. Showy lady's slipper, the taller species, grows 1½ to 3 feet high and bears as many as three 2- to 3-inch-wide flowers to a stem. The flowers are pure white or white flushed with rose. White down covers the stems and the 8-inch-long leaves.

HOW TO GROW. In general, lady's slippers need shade and acid soil. Pink lady's slipper, difficult to domesticate, grows in Zones 3-8. It requires a well-drained, very acid soil and grows best in deep leaf mold. Showy lady's slipper, hardy in Zones 4-7, does best in wet, neutral to slightly acid swamps and bogs. In both cases, propagation by using seeds is very difficult, as is transplanting from the wild. Instead, set out nursery-grown plants in the fall. Set the rhizomes of pink lady's slipper 1 to 1½ inches deep; those of showy lady's slipper only ½ inch deep. Space plants 1 to 2 feet apart. Mulch plants lightly with dry leaves or pine needles. Lady's slippers should not be moved; established plants bloom best.

D

DAY LILY See *Hemerocallis*

DENNSTAEDTIA

D. punctilobula (hay-scented fern, boulder fern)

Among the easiest ferns to grow, the hay-scented fern not only tolerates dry, moist or swampy soils but thrives in deep, medium or open shade. This hardy fern spreads quickly by means of underground stems, or rhizomes, creating a dense cover of light-green, deciduous foliage that can be used in difficult situations—on steep slopes, for example, or in the perpetual shade of house foundations. In spring the hay-scented fern sends up curled leaf buds covered with silver-white hairs. As the lance-shaped fronds unfold, these hairs will cover the stalks and stems and, when the plants are crushed, give off the scent of new-mown hay. The arching fronds, 11 inches wide, are covered with pairs of leaflets that turn brown in fall. The spores are held by cuplike membranes found at intervals along the leaflets.

HOW TO GROW. The hay-scented fern is hardy in Zones 3-8. It does best in a moist, well-drained slightly acid soil composed of 1 part loam, 1 part coarse sand and 2 parts leaf mold or peat moss. A mulch of leaves or evergreen boughs will help retain moisture while protecting roots during the winter. Plant hay-scented ferns in spring, setting them 1 inch deep and 2 feet apart. Fertilize each spring by spreading bone meal at the base of the fern at the rate of 1 ounce per square yard; or use fish emulsion fertilizer diluted to half the strength recommended. Remove dead fronds in early spring before new growth appears. Propagate from spores collected in late summer or fall, or by root division in early spring before new leaf buds appear.

DICENTRA

D. cucullaria (Dutchman's breeches), *D. spectabilis* (common bleeding heart)

Dutchman's breeches, a native American perennial wildflower, and common bleeding heart, a favorite old-fashioned garden perennial, both thrive in the medium to intermittent shade of deciduous trees, as long as they have filtered sunlight in early spring. Both species have finely divided fernlike foliage and spring flowers.

The delicate arching foliage of Dutchman's breeches grows 6 to 10 inches tall. Arching spikes of nodding white flowers are borne from mid- to late spring. Each flower, ½ to ⅔ inch long, is white, tipped in yellow, with two spurs that give it a resemblance to pantaloons hung upside down. Its foliage also dies down by midsummer. Common bleeding heart bears its

HAY-SCENTED FERN
Dennstaedtia punctilobula

DUTCHMAN'S BREECHES
Dicentra cucullaria

For climate zones and frost dates, see maps, pages 152-153.

DICHONDRA
Dichondra repens

gracefully pendant 1-inch flowers on arching 8- to 10-inch flower stems. Blooming from mid- to late spring, the deep pink flowers are heart-shaped. The variety Alba has white flowers. The blue-green foliage forms mounds 2½ to 3 feet tall and equally broad. By midsummer the foliage often shrivels away, returning the following spring.

Dutchman's breeches multiplies naturally and is excellent for use in areas of open woodland. Common bleeding heart makes an excellent specimen plant in a perennial flower border, or it can be planted among ferns, hostas, gypsophilas and other plants that will fill in when the foliage fades.

HOW TO GROW. Common bleeding heart is hardy in Zones 4-8, but it does not do well in Florida or along the Gulf Coast. In Zones 4-7, plants are very long-lived, lasting 20 years or more; in Zones 8 and 9, plants last only a few years because of summer heat. Dutchman's breeches is hardy in Zones 4-8. Plant common bleeding heart in spring in well-drained soil enriched with peat moss or leaf mold, setting plants 2 to 2½ feet apart. Keep the soil moist in the summer; a mulch helps and also keeps the soil cool. Dutchman's breeches grow best in loose, humusy, slightly acid soil that is well drained. In soil that is too acid, the plants will produce leaves but few flowers. Set the roots 4 to 6 inches apart and 1 to 1½ inches deep. Dust an all-purpose fertilizer around both species of plants in early spring. Mulch both in winter. Bleeding heart may be propagated from seeds sown in the fall; they will bloom the following year. Or start stem or root cuttings in the spring. Established plants should not be disturbed; divide them only if they become overcrowded. Seeds of Dutchman's breeches can be sown in summer, or the fleshy roots can be divided in fall.

DICHONDRA

D. repens, also called *D. micrantha* (dichondra, lawn leaf)

Widely grown as a substitute for lawn grass in the Southwest, dichondra flourishes in open shade where many grasses cannot survive. Its tiny leaves, ¼ to ½ inch wide, look like a sea of overlapping lily pads. It can grow as tall as 6 inches, but if walked on frequently, plants may be less than 1 inch tall; in moderate foot traffic they become 1½ to 2 inches tall. Dichondra can also be kept at any height by mowing. It spreads rapidly by underground runners and by seeding itself. A perennial, dichondra is also useful for filling cracks between flagstones and for edging borders.

HOW TO GROW. Dichondra is hardy in Zones 9 and 10; it tolerates temperatures down to 25° but should not be walked on if leaves are frosted because this will kill plants. Prepare soil as for lawn grass, adding a 2- to 3-inch layer of leaf mold or peat moss to the top 6 inches of soil and supplementing this with two to three pounds of nitrogen-rich fertilizer per 1,000 square feet. Sow seeds or set out plugs of sod any time from spring through midfall, although midspring is best. For a lawn, sow seeds at the rate of one to two pounds per 1,000 square feet; set plugs of sod 6 to 12 inches apart. Keep moist while seedlings or plugs are growing and, once established, continue to water frequently. A seeded dichondra lawn will take six to eight weeks to become established; one started from plugs five to six weeks. For a rich green color, feed every three months with a nitrogen-rich fertilizer.

DIGITALIS

D. purpurea (foxglove)

Given cool growing conditions and protection from wind, foxgloves will bloom in open or intermittent shade almost as effectively as in sun. Often used as a border or background plant, foxgloves for many years were grown as biennials—

FOXGLOVE
Digitalis purpurea

that is, they produced vegetative growth the first year and flowers the second. Hybridization has developed a strain called Foxy that blooms the first year as well as the second. It is a tall plant, 2 to 3 feet high, with long, narrow leaves concentrated in a rosette at the base of the stem and smaller, sparser leaves along the stem. The flowers are borne in 1-foot spikes; they are closely spaced, nodding, tubular in shape, and 2 to 3 inches long. Flower colors include white, cream, yellow, rose, red, magenta and purple, and many have spotted throats. Each plant of Foxy produces 9 to 10 flower stalks. The leaves of foxgloves are poisonous; a chemical in them is used in producing a heart stimulant, digitalis.

HOW TO GROW. Foxgloves grow in Zones 5-8 in rich, well-drained soil to which compost or peat moss has been added. For spring or early summer flowers, sow seeds of Foxy hybrids outdoors in the fall; they need five months to come into bloom. Or sow them indoors six to eight weeks before the last frost and set them outdoors as soon as the ground can be cultivated. Space seedlings 12 to 18 inches apart. Fertilize monthly with an all-purpose garden fertilizer. Foxgloves often reproduce themselves from their own scattered seed.

DOGWOOD See *Cornus*
DRAGONROOT See *Arisaema*
DROOPING LEUCOTHOË See *Leucothoë*
DUTCHMAN'S PIPE See *Aristolochia*
DWARF LILY-TURF See *Ophiopogon*
DUTCHMAN'S BREECHES See *Dicentra*

E

ENKIANTHUS

E. campanulatus (redvein enkianthus); *E. perulatus*, also called *E. japonicus* (white enkianthus)

Both the height and the spreading symmetrical growth of these tall deciduous shrubs recommend them as specimen plants for a garden in intermittent shade, but they are also often used as background plantings for azaleas, whose needs are similar. In spring the enkianthuses produce drooping clusters of small white to pale orange bell-shaped flowers at the ends of their branches; these open well before the oval leaves appear and last until the leaves are fully formed. In fall the foliage turns fiery orange-red, a color that is deepened if the plant is exposed during this period to the sun.

Redvein enkianthus may reach a height of 8 feet in cold regions and as much as 30 feet in mild areas, branching out in open tiers to a width about two thirds of its height. Its waxy flowers, ½ inch long, are cream colored, yellow or pale orange, veined and tipped with pink or red; they form loose clusters up to 3 inches wide. The leaves are dull green with serrated edges and grow up to 3 inches long.

White enkianthus seldom reaches more than 6 feet tall. Its growth is more broadly rounded than that of the red-veined species and its leaves are smaller, 2 inches or less in length, with rounded serrations. The white flowers, about ½ inch long, bloom in tight round 2-inch clusters a week or so in advance of the other plant. Fewer nurseries stock the white enkianthus, but the smaller plant's deeper red fall foliage make it a plant worth searching for.

HOW TO GROW. Redvein and white enkianthus are both hardy in Zones 5-8. Both species require soil that is moist, well drained and quite acid, enriched with peat moss or leaf mold. Set out young plants in spring or fall, allowing enough distance between them and other plants or structures to accommodate their eventual spread. Keep the soil moist during dry spells. Propagate from stem cuttings, or by soil layering—fastening a branch to the ground until it takes root.

REDVEIN ENKIANTHUS
Enkianthus campanulatus

For climate zones and frost dates, see maps, pages 152-153.

BISHOP'S HAT
Epimedium grandiflorum

WINTER ACONITE
Eranthis hyemalis

EPIMEDIUM

E. grandiflorum, also called *E. macranthum* (bishop's hat, long-spurred epimedium); *E. pinnatum* (Persian epimedium)

Whatever the density of shade, open to deep, the delicate-looking epimediums will thrive, growing slowly to eventually form clumps 9 to 12 inches tall. The leathery heart-shaped leaves of this perennial are 2 to 3 inches long, tinged red when they unfold, changing to light green in summer and to bronze in fall. In late spring the plants bear multicolored flower sprays on wiry stems. Bishop's hat has red, purple and white flowers up to 2 inches wide with long spurs. Persian epimedium has ½- to ¾-inch-wide bright yellow flowers with short spurs, and on one variant, *E. pinnatum colchicum,* the flowers have darker yellow centers. Both species make excellent ground covers beneath trees, along wooded paths or tucked in the rock garden.

HOW TO GROW. Bishop's hat and Persian epimediums are hardy in Zones 4-8; they do best in moist, well-drained soil supplemented with peat moss or leaf mold. Set out new plants in spring or fall, spacing them 8 to 10 inches apart. Provide a permanent mulch, 3 to 4 inches deep, of wood chips, ground bark or chunky peat moss to maintain moisture and keep out weeds. In the early spring, before new foliage appears, cut plants back to the ground to remove dead growth of the previous year. Propagate additional epimediums by dividing plants in fall or spring.

ERANTHIS

E. hyemalis (winter aconite)

Planted in large clusters of 25 or more, the cold-weather winter aconite forms a yellow carpet in late winter or early spring, in the open shade of a house wall where it receives weak sunlight in the early morning or late afternoon, or under the branches of birch trees, witch hazel, or pussy willow. It also thrives in rock gardens, combining well with snowdrops, two-leaved squills and crocuses, and it can be grown in containers.

This hardy tuberous plant grows only 2 to 4 inches high, each stem producing a single yellow flower 1 inch across; the flowers resemble buttercups and have a honey-like aroma. They are surrounded by collars of finely cut green or bronze-green foliage that lasts about six weeks after the flowers fade, disappearing finally in midsummer.

HOW TO GROW. Winter aconites are hardy in Zones 5-9 but need protection from wind. Plant them in late summer or early fall, soaking the tubers in water for 24 hours before putting them in the ground. Set them 2 to 3 inches deep and space them 3 to 4 inches apart. Keep the soil moist during the first autumn after they are planted.

Propagate additional winter aconites by replanting whole clumps rather than individual tubers. The clumps can be moved safely even when they are in flower, as long as some soil remains around their roots. Winter aconite spreads rapidly and will also seed itself, producing seedlings that will flower in two to three years.

ERYTHRONIUM

E. americanum (yellow adder's-tongue lily, trout lily, amber-bell); *E. grandiflorum* (fawn lily, lamb's tongue, avalanche lily, snow lily, Easter bells); *E.* 'Pagoda' (Pagoda fawn lily); *E. purpurascens* (Sierra fawn lily)

Found wild in woodlands of all areas of the United States except the Deep South, these small lilies, with mottled leaves and dainty flowers, take naturally to the open shade of springtime. All of them bear pleasantly scented 1- to 3-inch flowers of similar shape, but they are known by many different names. Sometimes called fawn lilies because of the dappled coloring in their leaves, they are also called trout lilies in areas where their bloom coincides with the opening of trout season, or Easter bells in the central Rockies where they bloom around Easter time. Wherever they grow, their season of bloom is generally midspring. They are most effective scattered informally among tall deciduous trees, by a pool or along a shaded path.

The yellow adder's-tongue lily spreads rapidly from offsets of the bulblike corms and grows 1 foot high. It has purple-brown and white mottled leaves and yellow flowers with brown centers sometimes tinged with pink. The fawn lily, tallest of this group, eventually grows 2 feet high. Its leaves are a shining, unmottled green, and its golden-yellow flowers have dark red or maroon centers. It spreads more slowly than the yellow adder's-tongue lily. Pagoda fawn lily is a dwarf, never more than 8 inches high, with unmottled green foliage and brown-centered pale yellow flowers. Sierra fawn lily has unmottled light-green leaves with fluted or wavy edges and light yellow-green flowers tinged with purple.

HOW TO GROW. All these lilies are hardy in Zones 3-9, but the fawn lily and Sierra fawn lily are difficult to grow at low altitudes, preferring a mountainous setting. They do best in a moist, well-drained soil rich in leaf mold; unlike other bulbs, they need watering in summer. Plant the bulbous corms 4 to 6 inches apart and cover them with 2 to 3 inches of soil. Use a mulch of wood chips or pine bark 2 inches thick to retain moisture, and replenish it every two to three years in the autumn. Propagate new plants by dividing the corms in summer or fall, using the small offsets growing beside the larger corms; replant young and old corms immediately.

EUONYMUS
E. fortunei coloratus (purple winter creeper)

One of the most colorful of the evergreen vines, purple winter creeper thrives in intermittent or open shade. Its ½- to 2-inch-long leaves grow on trailing stems that root as they move along the surface, making a dense carpet up to 6 inches tall. In fall and winter, the foliage is tinged with reddish-purple. There are no flowers or fruit. Purple winter creeper, which is widely used to control erosion on sloping banks, is also a valuable plant for rocky ground or for hiding unsightly tree stumps.

HOW TO GROW. Purple winter creeper is hardy in Zones 5-8, and does best in well-drained soil enriched with 1 part peat moss or leaf mold for every 2 parts of soil. Set out plants in spring or fall, spacing them 1 to 2 feet apart. Between plants, add a permanent mulch, 2 to 3 inches deep, of wood chips, ground bark or chunky peat moss. Propagate from cuttings or by dividing plants in spring or early fall.

F

FALSE SPIREA See *Astilbe*
FAWN LILY See *Erythronium*
FESCUE See *Festuca*

FESTUCA
F. arundinacea, also called *F. elatior* (tall fescue, meadow fescue); *F. ovina glauca* (blue fescue); *F. rubra* (red fescue)

Several of the fescues, meadow grasses that grow in even the poorest soils, flourish in open to medium shade, depending on the species grown. For bright color, however, they need some sun during the day. Tall fescue forms clumps of medium green leaves 6 to 12 inches tall in open shade; it is often planted to prevent erosion on banks. Among the varieties frequently recommended for shade are Alta, Goar and

PAGODA FAWN LILY
Erythronium 'Pagoda'

PURPLE WINTER CREEPER
Euonymous fortunei coloratus

For climate zones and frost dates, see maps, pages 152-153.

BLUE FESCUE
Festuca ovina glauca

LARGE FOTHERGILLA
Fothergilla major

Kentucky-31. Blue fescue grows in tufted mounds, 4 to 10 inches tall, in open shade; it bears blue-purple seed-filled spikes. It is an ornamental grass, often used in clumps in the garden or to edge the borders of flower beds. Red fescues, often used in shady lawns, come in two forms: some grow in clumps up to 3 feet tall, while others spread across the ground. Both thrive in open shade and have stiff, dark leaves and reddish-purple seed-filled spikes. Noteworthy types recommended for shade are Chewings fescue and the Illahee, Pennlawn and Rainier varieties of creeping red fescue.

HOW TO GROW. Fescue grasses are hardy in Zones 4-9, but do best in cool climates. They will grow in almost any soil. Most fescues prefer moist, well-drained soil, neutral or slightly alkaline, but blue fescue produces the most vivid color in poor, fairly dry soil. Plants tolerate wind, sand and salty sea air. Sow tall fescue seeds in early fall; to minimize space between clumps, sow seeds at the rate of four to eight pounds per 1,000 square feet. Sow red fescue at the rate of three to five pounds per 1,000 square feet in early fall or early spring. Plant the decorative blue fescue in clumps in spring or fall, spacing the clumps 6 to 12 inches apart, depending on the thickness desired. Provide a light mulch of wood chips, ground bark or chunky peat moss between clumps to keep out weeds. Fertilize fescues in late spring and fall, using a nitrogen-rich lawn fertilizer. For lawns, mow to a height of 2½ inches; in very hot weather, keep 3 inches tall.

FETTERBUSH See *Leucothoë*
FIVE-FINGER FERN See *Adiantum*
FORGET-ME-NOT See *Myosotis*

FOTHERGILLA

F. gardenii (dwarf fothergilla, witch alder); *F. major* (large fothergilla)

A native of the southeastern United States, the fothergillas are deciduous shrubs that grow best in intermittent or open shade. They range from sprawling mounds less than 3 feet tall to slender treelike pyramids more than 9 feet tall. The fragrant white flower heads, 1 to 2 inches long, resemble shaving brushes and consist solely of stamens, without petals. In fall the leaves turn brilliant red, yellow and orange.

Dwarf fothergilla grows only 2 to 3 feet tall and spreads up to 4 feet. Its flower heads, 1½ inches long, appear in early spring long before the 2½-inch-long leaves unfold. Large fothergilla may grow 9 feet tall and 4 to 6 feet wide. It bears 2-inch flower heads at the same time as the leaves unfurl; its leaves grow up to 4 inches long. Both fothergillas are especially effective in front of evergreens, whose dark hues set off the spring flowers and fall foliage.

HOW TO GROW. Fothergillas are hardy in Zones 5-9, and do best in a moist, cool, well-drained acid soil consisting of 1 part of peat moss or leaf mold to every 2 parts of soil. They need protection from the wind, and in the northernmost sections of the growing zones their roots should be protected from cold with a permanent mulch, 3 to 4 inches deep, of wood chips, ground bark or chunky peat moss. Propagate from cuttings of new growth taken in late spring or early summer, or from root cuttings taken in the spring or fall.

FOXGLOVE See *Digitalis*
FRINGE TREE See *Chionanthus*

FRITILLARIA

F. lanceolata (narrow-leaved fritillary, riceroot fritillary); *F. meleagris* (checkered fritillary, guinea-hen flower, snake's head); *F. recurva* (scarlet fritillary)

The spring-flowering fritillaries open their many-colored boldly patterned blooms in the filtered light of open shade like that of the woodlands to which they are accustomed; most of them are western wildflowers, but the checkered fritillary grows throughout North America. These bulb plants are effective in rock gardens, on shaded slopes, along stream beds, and can also be grown in containers placed in subdued light on patios and terraces.

All of the fritillaries bear nodding bell-shaped flowers, sometimes singly, sometimes in ringlike clusters that spring from the tips of the stems. In the narrow-leaved fritillary, which grows 1 to 2 feet tall, these clusters are shaded by a series of whorls of shiny leaves. The flowers themselves are 1½ inches long, mottled purple and yellow with thin purple stripes, and their petals turn in at the tips, like claws. The checkered fritillary grows 1 foot tall, with narrow, pointed gray-green leaves and distinctive checkered-patterned flowers of purple and white that resemble the speckled plumage of the guinea hen. The flowers are 2 inches long and are borne singly or in groups of three. The scarlet fritillary, taller than the others, reaches a height of 24 to 30 inches, and has bronze-green leaves that grow in whorls near the middle of the stem. Its scarlet flowers, 1½ inches long, are checkered with yellow inside and striped with purple outside, and appear either singly or in a terminal group of three or four above the leaves.

HOW TO GROW. The checkered fritillary is hardy in Zones 3-10, the narrow-leaved fritillary in Zones 6-10, the scarlet fritillary in Zones 7-10. All of them do best in a light, well-drained soil amply supplied with humus. Plant the bulbs in late summer or early fall, setting them in the ground 3 to 4 inches deep and 3 to 4 inches apart. Fertilize them with an all-purpose 5-10-5 garden fertilizer dug in at planting time and sprinkled on the surface of the soil each year as soon as new growth appears. Water fritillaries plentifully during their period of active growth. Propagate by digging up the bulbs in early summer, after the foliage dies; separate the smaller bulbs that form around the large ones and replant them immediately. Fritillaries also seed themselves, but they take four to six years to bloom.

FRITILLARY See *Fritillaria*
FUNKIA See *Hosta*

G

GALAX

G. aphylla, also called *G. urceolata* (galax, wandflower, wand plant)

Galax is an evergreen ground cover that thrives in every sort of shade, open to deep. Its shiny heart-shaped leaves, ½ to 5 inches wide, create a thick mat 4 to 6 inches tall. Except when it is planted in very deep shade where the sun never penetrates, the serrated foliage turns purple or bronze in fall or winter. From late spring to midsummer, tiny white flowers, less than ¼ inch wide, line flower stems 1 to 2 feet tall. Galax spreads moderately fast on creeping underground stems, and it is often planted under azaleas and rhododendrons or in rock gardens.

HOW TO GROW. Galax is hardy in Zones 4-8. It does best in a cool, moist, well-drained acid soil. To improve drainage and aeration, add 1 part of peat moss or leaf mold and 1 part builder's sand for every 2 parts of soil. Keep the soil moist, if necessary providing a permanent mulch, 2 or 3 inches deep, of leaf mold or pine needles. In Zones 5 and 6, set out plants in spring or fall, spacing them about 12 inches apart; in Zones 7 and 8, set them out at any time. Propagate by

CHECKERED FRITILLARY
Fritillaria meleagris

GALAX
Galax aphylla

For climate zones and frost dates, see maps, pages 152-153.

WINTERGREEN
Gaultheria procumbens

SPOTTED GERANIUM
Geranium maculatum

dividing roots in early spring or in early fall. Galax may also be started from seed in late fall or winter, but it takes a year or two to become established.

GARDEN BALSAM See *Impatiens*

GAULTHERIA
G. procumbens (wintergreen, checkerberry, tea berry)

Wintergreen forms an evergreen carpet in open or dappled shade, provided it is planted under high-branching trees where some sun filters through to stimulate the production of flowers and berries. The plants grow 2 to 6 inches tall, and bear clusters of leathery leaves 1 to 2 inches long on woody stems. Colorful throughout the year, the leaves are red in spring as they unfold, become shiny green in summer, and turn bronze in fall. Waxy white or pink bell-shaped flowers, ¼ inch long, dangle from the stem tips in summer, followed by mint-flavored red berries, ¼ to ½ inch wide, which remain until the following spring. When crushed, the leaves give off a spicy aroma. Wintergreen spreads by underground runners and is often used with mosses in woodland gardens because their soil needs are similar.

HOW TO GROW. Wintergreen is hardy in Zones 4-8 and does best in a moist, well-drained, very acid soil. To improve drainage, mix in 1 part leaf mold or peat moss for every 2 parts of soil. Set out nursery plants in early spring or fall, spacing them 1 to 2 feet apart. Keep the ground moist until plants are established. Provide a permanent mulch, 2 or 3 inches deep, of leaf mold or pine needles to retain soil moisture. Additional wintergreen plants can be propagated by dividing the thick roots, by stem cuttings or from seeds— but the last two methods are difficult, and it may be simpler to buy new plants.

GERANIUM
G. maculatum (spotted geranium, wild geranium)

A distant relative of the familiar cultivated house plant, the wild geranium takes easily to open shade, but it does need a location sheltered from the wind. This 1- to 2-foot-high perennial has an open, branching habit of growth that combines well with ferns and makes it especially suitable for informal woodland settings. The deeply cut leaves, 3 to 5 inches wide, are rough and hairy and have toothed edges. The lavender-pink five-petaled flowers, ½ to 1 inch across, bloom in loose clusters in spring and early summer, and are followed by long, tapering seed pods which burst open when the seed is ripe, scattering it several feet away. Wild geraniums spread rapidly on plump underground stems.

HOW TO GROW. Wild geraniums are hardy in Zones 4-8 and grow best in rich, moist, slightly acid soil. Plant nursery-grown plants in the early spring, spacing them 10 to 14 inches apart. Mulch them lightly with leaves to conserve moisture. Propagate additional plants from root cuttings taken in the spring or fall, setting the cuttings 1 inch deep, or from seeds sown as soon as they ripen. Seedlings will bloom in two or three years.

GERANIUM, STRAWBERRY See *Saxifraga*
GINGER, WILD See *Asarum*
GOLDEN POLYPODY See *Polypodium*
GOUTWEED, SILVEREDGE See *Aegopodium*
GRAPE, OREGON HOLLY See *Mahonia*
GRAPE HYACINTH See *Muscari*
GREEN-DRAGON See *Arisaema*
GROUND-HEMLOCK See *Taxus*
GUINEA-HEN FLOWER See *Fritillaria*

H

HAW, BLACK See *Viburnum*
HAY-SCENTED FERN See *Dennstaedtia*

HEDERA

H. helix (English ivy); *H. colchica* (Persian ivy)

These evergreen ivies, with their familiar dark green year-round foliage, prefer open or intermittent shade to full sun, which in winter can burn their leaves. They and many other varieties of English ivy are ideal for covering shaded banks, for carpeting the foreground of border plantings, and for sheathing fences, posts and tree stumps.

English ivy produces a dense carpet of leathery dark green foliage; the triangular leaves have three to five lobes and are 2 to 4 inches long. It climbs 50 to 100 feet by attaching aerial roots to any coarse surface. Persian ivy climbs rapidly to a height of 20 to 30 feet by the same means. Its thick oval or heart-shaped leaves are dull dark green, 4 to 6 inches wide and 8 to 10 inches long—and are especially effective against red brick. Two varieties of Persian ivy are Dentata, with narrow leaves that are slightly toothed, and Variegata, with leaves streaked with a creamy yellow or pale green. When ivies reach their full height and can climb no farther, they produce adult heart-shaped leaves without lobes, and bear yellow-green flowers, 1½ to 2½ inches wide, followed by clusters of black pea-sized fruit.

HOW TO GROW. English ivy is hardy in Zones 5-9; Persian ivy in Zones 7-9. Both do well in any moist, well-drained garden soil that is neutral or slightly acid. Plant vines in early spring, setting them 1 to 2 feet apart. Keep soil moist but not soggy; ivy used as a ground cover will benefit from a mulch of straw until it becomes established. Fertilize each spring by dusting all-purpose fertilizer around the base of each vine. Prune climbing ivy in early spring, cutting vines close to their support and removing dead leaves. Ground-covering ivy need not be pruned except to contain its growth. Propagate from stem cuttings of ivy that has touched the ground and taken root or start cuttings in moist vermiculite.

HEDYOTIS See *Houstonia*

HELLEBORUS

H. niger (Christmas rose); *H. orientalis* (Lenten rose)

Good plants to grow near a step or doorway where their flowers will be readily noticed, both the Christmas and Lenten roses thrive in open shade, preferring it to sun. Neither is truly a rose, and both are evergreen if given protection from northern and western winds. They grow 12 to 15 inches tall and have shiny, dark green leathery leaves that are divided into seven to nine segments. The Christmas rose blooms between late fall and early spring, depending on the climate. Each flower stalk bears a single 2- to 4-inch white bloom, sometimes tinged with pink. The center of the flower has numerous yellow pollen-bearing stamens. Durable and able to withstand cold temperatures, the flowers generally last a month, but their beauty can be prolonged for up to three months by protecting them from snow and ice with a temporary plastic-covered frame. One variety, Altifolius, has larger flowers, up to 5 inches across.

The Lenten rose blooms later, usually between early and midspring, producing 2-inch flowers that may be cream-colored, chocolate brown, purple, or sometimes green. Several blooms are borne on each flower stem. The variety Atrorubens has flowers that are brownish-purple on the outside and greenish-purple on the inside; one group of Lenten roses, the Millet hybrids, have solid, dotted or striped flowers rang-

ENGLISH IVY
Hedera helix

For climate zones and frost dates, see maps, pages 152-153.

CHRISTMAS ROSE
Helleborus niger

DAY LILY
Hemerocallis hybrid

ing in color from white to pink, red or brown. The roots of both Christmas and Lenten roses are poisonous.

HOW TO GROW. Christmas roses are hardy in Zones 4-8; Lenten roses in Zones 4-9. They do best in a cool, moist environment and in a well-drained neutral to slightly alkaline soil that has been generously enriched with peat moss, leaf mold, or compost. Set plants in the ground in the spring, spacing them 12 to 15 inches apart. Stretch the roots down rather than spreading them out and place the crown, where stem and roots join, 1 inch below the surface of the soil. Mulch plants with a 1-inch layer of compost, which should be renewed every spring. Also, every spring remove old, unattractive foliage and feed plants with a balanced fertilizer, such as 10-10-10. Every three or four years, scratch a handful of ground limestone into the soil around the plants. Both of these roses are slow to become established, and should not be divided. Additional plants can be started from seeds sown indoors in early fall, but it takes three or four years for them to reach flowering size.

HEMEROCALLIS
H. hybrids (day lily)

Highly adaptable perennials, day lilies can tolerate open to deep shade but bloom best where they receive some sun. Afternoon shade is necessary, however, where the summer climate is hot. Day lilies form thick clumps of arching grasslike foliage. The trumpet-shaped lily-like flowers range in color from pale cream to yellow and orange, plus red, pink and mahogany. They may be bicolored, with eyes of a contrasting color, or polychromed, with petals of blended related shades. From the thousands of varieties developed, with different flowering periods, selections can be made to provide flowers from spring to frost. Pink and other light shades, which tend to bleach in the sun, are especially good for shade gardens. The size range of available plants is also large, from dwarf varieties growing 15 to 18 inches tall to giants reaching 4 or more feet in height. Flower size ranges from 3 inches across to 8 inches or more; there may be a single or double row of petals. Some varieties have evergreen foliage when grown where winters are mild. Use day lilies as specimen plants or massed in borders, alone or in combination with other perennials. They compete well with tree roots and can be used along the top or at the base of a wall, in front of a fence, beside ponds or streams, on slopes or as a ground cover. Easy to grow, they multiply freely and are seldom bothered by pests.

HOW TO GROW. Day lilies are hardy in Zones 3-9. Many varieties have been developed for specific regions; check with a local nurseryman for those best suited to your area. Day lilies grow in any good well-drained garden soil. To improve soil drainage, work organic matter such as peat moss or compost into the soil when planting. Also add a handful of bone meal for each plant. Space plants 1 to 2 feet apart, depending on their mature size. Spread out the roots in the planting hole rather than placing them straight down. Set the crown, where stem and roots meet, 1 inch below the soil surface. If the weather is dry during the plant's period of flowering, water thoroughly. Feed in early spring with an all-purpose fertilizer such as 5-10-5. Mulch around newly planted day lilies to conserve moisture. A winter mulch of straw or salt hay also helps to keep plants from being heaved out of the ground and in northern areas protects them from severe cold. Remove flower stems that have completed blooming. Propagate additional plants from divisions at any time during the growing season. Divide plants when overcrowded, usually after four to six years of flowering.

HEMLOCK See *Tsuga*
HEMLOCK, GROUND See *Taxus*
HOLLY See *Ilex*
HONEYSUCKLE See *Lonicera*

HOSTA (FUNKIA)

H. lancifolia 'Kabitan'; *H. plantaginea* (August lily); *H.* 'Royal Standard'; *H. sieboldiana; H. undulata* 'Medio-picta' (all called hosta)

Whatever the shade in a garden, dappled to dense, open to covered, there is a hosta that will thrive in it. These durable perennials with their pointed oval or heart-shaped leaves form handsome mounds of foliage from 15 inches up to 6 feet wide, depending on the length of the leaves. Deeply veined and in some species wavy-edged, hosta leaves come in a variety of greens that shade gardeners can mix or match: golden yellow to pale green to deep jade, and variegated patterns of yellow, green and white. Variegated hostas develop their best color when grown in medium or intermittent shade. There are also hostas with dusty blue-green leaves, such as *H. sieboldiana,* but these are recommended only for open shade, as they may lose their blue coloration when grown without enough light.

Clumps of hosta last up to 20 years without division or special care. Their adaptability and great range of sizes make them useful as ground covers, as plants for the foreground or background of a perennial border or as single specimen plants. While not grown specifically for their flowers, all hostas except those grown in dense shade bear clusters of bell-shaped white to lavender or blue flowers on spikes 18 inches to 9 feet tall. Because hostas cross pollinate easily and are extensively hybridized in Japan, from which many are being imported, there is some overlap in the names of species and hybrids available commercially; gardeners should buy plants from reputable mail-order sources or examine plants in a nursery to ensure getting the colors and leaf shapes they want.

The narrow 5-inch leaves of *H. lancifolia* Kabitan have wavy margins and retain their bright yellow color throughout the growing season; purple flowers bloom in late summer. Kabitan is a useful rock garden plant in Zones 3-9.

The August lily is an old-fashioned hosta with 10-inch yellow-green leaves, recommended as a ground cover plant in Zones 3-9. It is renowned for the fragrance of its white flower bells, which bloom in August. Royal Standard, a hybrid offspring of the August lily, adds extreme hardiness to the fragrance of its parent; this hosta survives below-freezing temperatures from Zone 3 southward and will grow in any amount of light from full sun to deep shade. *H. undulata* Medio-picta has silvery white markings along the centers of its 15-inch wavy leaves; these variegations are most pronounced on plants grown in the shade. The Medio-picta hosta is hardy in Zones 3-9; its lavender flowers bloom in summer on 12-inch spikes.

HOW TO GROW. Plant hostas 12 to 24 inches apart, depending on their size, in any moist but well-drained garden soil enriched with compost or leaf mold. Water during dry spells. Clumps can be left undisturbed indefinitely or divided in early spring. Hostas reseed themselves easily; to prevent spreading, remove faded flowers before they go to seed.

HOUSTONIA

H. caerulea, also called *Hedyotis caerulea* (bluets, Quaker ladies, innocence)

A harbinger of spring, tiny star-shaped bluets thrive in open shade, naturalizing to form a flowering carpet in wood-

HOSTA
Hosta undulata 'Medio-picta'

For climate zones and frost dates, see maps, pages 152-153.

land gardens where the soil is moist. The dainty flowers, ½ inch across, have four pale blue petals shading to white around yellow centers, each bloom capping a slender 2- to 8-inch stem above clumps of ½-inch leaves. Bluets spread rapidly by seed and by means of creeping roots to form a dense turf. They may invade a formal lawn but they are valued as a diminutive accent and ground cover in shade.

HOW TO GROW. Bluets are hardy in Zones 4-9, and do best in moist acid-to-neutral soil. Sow seeds in early spring or fall by scratching the soil and scattering the seed over the surface. Bluets may also be started from nursery-grown stock, which is occasionally available. Once established, clumps can be divided in the spring, before or after flowering.

HYACINTH, GRAPE See *Muscari*

HYDRANGEA

H. anomala petiolaris (climbing hydrangea); *H. arborescens grandiflora* 'Annabelle' (hills-of-snow hydrangea); *H. macrophylla hortensia* 'All Summer Beauty' (big-leaved hydrangea); *H. macrophylla* 'Silver Variegated Mariesii' (big-leaved hydrangea)

Although hydrangeas are often grown in full sun, their flowers last longer and hold their color better in medium to open shade; in full sun they tend to wilt, especially in dry weather. Their flowers, the plants' main attraction, grow in large delicate clusters of white, pink or blue blooms characteristically composed of small starlike fertile flowers in the center surrounded on the outside by larger sterile flowers 1 to 1½ inches wide. The sterile flowers have four or five oval petals, the fertile flowers the same number of much smaller petals. Most hydrangeas are shrubs that grow 3 to 6 feet high and nearly as wide, but the climbing hydrangea is a vine, with twining stems and aerial roots that hold fast to rough surfaces, reaching a height of 15 to 50 feet. All these hydrangeas have pointed oval leaves with serrated edges, and all are perennial and deciduous.

The climbing hydrangea is most effective when climbing a tree trunk or shaded wall, where its lacy white flowers stand out prominently against a darker background. Its coarse-toothed leaves, 2 to 5 inches wide, are shiny and dark green on top, pale green and downy underneath. The flowers, starry in the center, larger-petaled outside, bloom in early summer in flat clusters 6 to 10 inches wide. In winter the shredding bark of older branches, red-brown in color, is also ornamental. Planted against a wall or trellis, the lateral branches of climbing hydrangea will spread to a width of 3 or 4 feet; when grown in the open, over a large rock or tree stump, the climbing hydrangea is bushy and compact.

Annabelle, a variety of the hills-of-snow hydrangea, bears 10-inch round clusters of pure white flowers almost all summer. The abundant blooms, all of them sterile, turn reddish brown as they fade and in warm climates remain on the shrub until pruned off. The fine-toothed leaves, 3 to 6 inches long, are bright green on top and slightly downy underneath. Annabelle grows 3 to 5 feet high and nearly as wide, and a row of them planted close together makes a fine informal border, especially when the flower-laden stems cascade over a low wall or fence.

Big-leaved hydrangeas have coarse-toothed shiny green leaves, 4 to 8 inches long, and grow 4 to 6 feet high and equally wide. All Summer Beauty has round flower clusters 4 to 8 inches wide composed mostly of large sterile flowers; it blooms throughout the summer. Silver Variegated Mariesii, whose leaves are edged in white, produces flat clusters of both sterile and fertile blooms, 4 to 6 inches wide, from

BLUETS
Houstonia caerulea

midsummer to early fall. The flowers of both plants are blue in acid soil, pink in alkaline soil.

HOW TO GROW. Climbing hydrangea and Annabelle are hardy in Zones 5-9, the big-leaved hydrangeas in Zones 6-10. All hydrangeas grow best in moist well-drained soil that has been enriched with compost. To acidify the soil at planting time for blue flowers on a big-leaved hydrangea, work 1 to 2 pounds of aluminum sulfate into it; to acidify it later, mix the same amount of aluminum sulfate with 7 gallons of water and apply around the plant in late winter or spring. To create an alkaline soil for pink flowers, work ground limestone into it, ¼ to ½ pound per plant, and each spring apply additional limestone to maintain the proper alkalinity.

Plant hydrangeas in fall or early spring. To grow Annabelle and big-leaved hydrangeas in a border, set plants 2 to 3 feet apart; to grow climbing hydrangea on a tree, dig a hole 3 feet by 3 feet at some distance from the tree—1 foot or more—and set the hydrangea into it; surround the hydrangea with a collar of metal or plastic 6 inches out from its stem to keep tree roots from interfering with the vine while it becomes established. Water during the growing season, but even when the plant is dormant never allow the soil to become thoroughly dry. Each spring, spread a layer of compost at the base of the plant. Feed with a liquid plant fertilizer every two weeks while flowers are in bloom.

Thin out weak or dead branches of climbing hydrangea after it has flowered and cut it back to contain growth. Prune Annabelle in early spring to encourage new growth, cutting back most stems to 2 feet from the ground; cut stems 3 years old or more to within 6 inches. Prune big-leaved hydrangeas after blooming to contain growth and remove weak branches.

Propagate hydrangeas from cuttings of new growth taken in late spring. Climbing and Annabelle hydrangeas can also be propagated by fastening stems against the ground until they take root. Annabelle hydrangea produces underground suckers that can be dug up and used to start new plants.

I

ILEX

I. aquifolium (English holly, common holly); *I. cornuta* 'Burfordii' (Burford holly); *I. crenata* (Japanese holly); *I. crenata* 'Convexa' (convex-leaf Japanese holly)

With their glossy green foliage and red, yellow or black berries, the broad-leaved evergreen hollies are exceptionally decorative plants, and they adapt well to many kinds of shade. English holly will tolerate deep shade; Burford holly, open shade; and Japanese holly, medium shade to full sun. Although they require very little care, most hollies bear fruit only on female plants and must be placed within 100 feet of male plants for pollination. Also, the berries in most species are borne only on the current year's growth, a factor that should be kept in mind when pruning and shaping them.

English holly, most commonly used for Christmas arrangements has prickly wide-toothed foliage, 1½ to 3 inches long, and bright red berries ¼ inch across. It normally grows 40 feet high; century-old holly trees sometimes become 100 feet tall. Frequently grown as a single specimen plant, when it is closely cropped it also makes a fine hedge under high-branched deciduous trees or between tall buildings. Burford, a fast-growing self-pollinating species, becomes 15 feet tall and has spineless leaves 2 to 3 inches long and unusually large ½-inch red berries. It too may be clipped as a hedge, and it is also used in border plantings or as a single specimen. The Japanese holly is a bushy shrub resembling boxwood. It bears small fine-toothed leaves, 1 inch long, and inconspicuous small black berries. Growing up to 10 feet high and

BIG-LEAVED HYDRANGEA
Hydrangea macrophylla 'Silver Variegated Mariesii'

ENGLISH HOLLY
Ilex aquifolium

For climate zones and frost dates, see maps, pages 152-153.

TOP: PATIENT LUCY, *Impatiens wallerana*
BOTTOM: GARDEN BALSAM, *I. balsamina*

CRESTED IRIS
Iris cristata

almost as wide, it can be pruned to much smaller dimensions and looks well when planted in combination with small deciduous trees. One of its many varieties, the convex-leaf Japanese holly, is dwarf and compact, becoming only 4 or 5 feet tall and very dense. Its leaves are only ½ inch long. It makes an excellent shrub under low windows or beside trellises and arbors.

HOW TO GROW. All hollies grow well in Zones 8 and 9, but the English and Japanese hollies will also survive in Zones 6 and 7. Hollies need a neutral to slightly acid soil, well-drained and fairly light and sandy. Plant them in early spring, before new growth begins; in the warmer regions they may also be planted in the fall. Feed them in early spring or late autumn with a fertilizer formulated for acid-loving broad-leaved evergreens. Water them during dry spells, especially the convex-leaf Japanese holly, which requires more moisture. Hollies are pruned only to shape them or to remove dead branches; they may be pruned in midwinter and their leaves and berries used for holiday decorations; midwinter pruning interferes least with their production of berries. Propagate from stem cuttings of new growth; they should produce berries in two to three years.

IMPATIENS

I. balsamina (garden balsam); *I. wallerana* (impatiens, patient Lucy)

Few annuals that grow in shade provide the range and intensity of color of impatiens. It flowers in all but deep shade and must actually have protection from hot afternoon sun to maintain its colors. Garden balsam, a staple in the border garden for many years, has long-lasting double flowers, up to 2½ inches across, of white, salmon, pink, purple, deep red or a combination of these. The plant has two distinct growth types. One, a tall variety, may reach 3 feet and branch very little; the flowers are produced along the stems. The other, a shorter type, forms 8- to 10-inch mounds of freely branching plants with the flowers displayed at the top. Both types have long, narrow, glossy, dark green leaves.

Impatiens was a leggy plant before extensive hybridization; newer varieties are compact multibranching plants, 6 to 18 inches tall and 10 to 24 inches across. Flat five-petaled flowers with thin, curving spurs are borne in clusters well above the foliage; colors range from red to scarlet, orange, rose, salmon, pink, white, purple, and bicolors. The leaves are glossy ovals. Impatiens is a tender perennial, hardy only in Zone 10; elsewhere it is treated as an annual.

HOW TO GROW. Both species do best in a rich, moist, sandy soil mulched to maintain adequate moisture. Sow seeds of garden balsam in the garden when all frost danger is past, or start them indoors four to six weeks before the last frost is due. When all danger of frost is past, set the plants in the garden, spacing tall-growing varieties 18 inches apart and compact varieties 8 to 10 inches apart.

Impatiens, which takes longer to germinate, should be started from seed indoors six to eight weeks before the last frost is due or purchased as seedlings. Set out 10 to 12 inches apart. It may also be propagated from stem cuttings. Pinch back garden balsam and impatiens to encourage bushiness, and feed monthly with an all-purpose fertilizer.

INNOCENCE See *Houstonia*
INTERRUPTED FERN See *Osmunda*

IRIS

I. cristata (dwarf crested iris, crested iris); *I. verna* (vernal iris, dwarf iris, violet iris)

Both these diminutive irises are woodland wildflowers, accustomed to open or intermittent shade. They grow from rhizomes—horizontal stems that spread along the surface of the ground—sending up fragrant flowers on short erect stalks amid narrow-bladed leaves that continue to grow after the flowers have faded. The delicacy of form and color so typical of cultivated irises is found in these irises, too. Three large outer segments, called sepals, spread out and slightly downward from the flower's base, while three petals grow erect; petals and sepals range from violet to white; sepals are marked near the bases with white, yellow or orange.

The dwarf crested iris is often used as a ground cover, particularly on steep slopes or banks. Though its foliage dies back in the fall, leaving the ground bare, the network of rhizomatic roots continues to anchor the soil. Under ideal conditions, rhizomes spread rapidly, multiplying the number of plants. Each rhizome produces about six leaves that are ¾ inch wide and may in the course of the summer become 12 inches long. One or two spicy-scented flowers grow from each plant on stalks 3 to 8 inches tall; the flowers are 2 inches wide and come in lilac-blue, mauve, purple or white with strongly ridged crests of white or yellow. Once established, dwarf crested irises bloom for many years.

Vernal iris is valued for its sweet scent and its miniature size, which makes it an ideal rock garden plant. Generally smaller than the dwarf crested iris, its flowers are only 1½ inches wide, and its flower stalks seldom more than 6 inches high. The leaves are less than ½ inch wide and about 6 inches long when the plant is in flower, elongating later to as much as 12 inches; they are covered on one side with bluish-white dust and as they age they become black and leathery. The flowers themselves are violet-blue to white, with lengthwise bands of yellow or orange marking the sepals.

HOW TO GROW. Dwarf crested iris, hardy in Zones 4-9, grows best in moist, well-drained slightly acid soil; vernal iris, hardy in Zones 5-9, needs moist sandy soil that is very acid. In Zones 5-7, set plants in the ground in early summer; in Zones 8 and 9 wait until early fall. Space the plants 6 to 12 inches apart, covering the rhizomes but leaving the tip of each plant visible at ground level. When grown between rocks, irises generally need no winter mulch, but in open ground a light covering of boughs or straw may be necessary to keep the shallow roots from heaving during northern winters. Propagate by dividing rhizomes when new growth begins in early spring; be sure that each division has at least one strong bud. Crested irises may reseed themselves.

IVY See *Hedera*

J

JACK-IN-THE-PULPIT See *Arisaema*
JAPANESE ANDROMEDA See *Pieris*
JAPANESE PAINTED FERN See *Athyrium*
JAPANESE ROSE See *Kerria*
JASMINE See *Jasminum*

JASMINUM

J. nudiflorum (winter jasmine); *J. officinale* (common white jasmine)

Although jasmines flower most abundantly in full sun, they are also amenable to open shade. The deciduous winter jasmine is a shrub with bright yellow flowers that is perhaps at its best planted along the top of a bank or a wall, where its arching stems can dip gracefully to the ground. If winter jasmine is allowed to grow freely, it reaches a height of 3 to 8 feet. However, if fastened to a thin support, it can be trained

COMMON WHITE JASMINE
Jasminum officinale

For climate zones and frost dates, see maps, pages 152-153.

to climb to a height of 15 feet, or it can be espaliered. Each compound leaf is composed of three glossy, deep green leaflets, oval in shape and 1 inch long. The flowers, which generally bloom in early spring in the north, appear singly and are 1 inch across, with five or six broadly oval petals. The variety Aureum has leaves that are marked with yellow.

The common white jasmine is more vinelike, with white star-shaped flowers that are best enjoyed when this evergreen vine is trained to climb over an arch, arbor or trellis. It climbs to a height of 30 feet with assistance, and its compound leaves are composed of five to seven leaflets, each ½ to 2½ inches long. The flowers are intensely fragrant and bloom in clusters of three to eight all summer long. Like winter jasmine, it too has a variety, Aureo-variegatum, with variegated yellow leaves. And there is also another variety, called Affine or Grandiflorum, with larger flowers, about 1¾ inches wide, tinged with pink.

HOW TO GROW. Winter jasmine is hardy in Zones 6-9 and in Zone 5 if sheltered from winter wind; common white jasmine is hardy in Zones 7-9. They thrive in any well-drained garden soil. As vines, jasmines should be planted 2 feet apart, but when winter jasmines are grown as shrubs, plants should be set 6 to 8 feet apart. Water during dry spells, and to help keep roots cool and moist, cover with a 2-inch mulch of wood chips or pine needles.

Each spring, scatter compost around the base of each plant. After it has flowered in the spring, winter jasmine may be cut back to within a few inches of the ground, as flowers for the following year will form on new growth produced during the summer. Thin out common white jasmine after flowering in the fall, but do not shorten. Propagate jasmine from stem cuttings taken in early spring or fall, rooting them in a mixture of peat moss and sand, or by fastening stems against the ground until they form roots.

JUDAS TREE See *Cercis*

K

KALMIA

K. latifolia (mountain laurel, calico bush)

Mountain laurel is an ideal plant for shade, preferring subdued light to sun; it will even do well in deep shade, although its bloom will be less abundant. This evergreen shrub, indigenous to the mountains of the eastern United States, grows 4 to 8 feet high but can be kept lower by pruning. Its glossy, oval, dark green leaves, 3 to 5 inches long, are almost hidden in late spring by masses of rose to white cup-shaped flowers which are borne in loose clusters 4 to 6 inches across. Inside these flowers the petals are marked with brown dots that look like sprinklings of nutmeg. A hardy plant, mountain laurel will keep its leaves unfurled even in severe cold. Mountain laurel spreads by sending up suckers. It does well near rhododendron, since both plants need acid soil. Use them for foundation plantings on the north side of a house, in woodland settings or behind spring-flowering bulbs in garden borders.

HOW TO GROW. Mountain laurel is hardy in Zones 5-9 and does best in a cool, moist, acid soil with peat moss or sand added. To retain moisture, give it a year-round 2- to 6-inch mulch of wood chips, ground bark, well-rotted oak leaves or pine needles. For greater bushiness and more abundant flowers, remove the mulch briefly in the spring and spread cottonseed meal or a fertilizer prepared for acid-loving plants around the base; then replace the mulch. The plant's flower production for the following year can be improved by pinching off the seed capsules when the flowers fade, but this is

MOUNTAIN LAUREL
Kalmia latifolia

not essential. If pruning is needed, do it immediately after flowering stops. If the plant dies back in winter, cut it to the ground; it will send up new growth.

KERRIA
K. japonica 'Argenteo-variegata' (variegated kerria); *K. japonica* 'Pleniflora' (globeflower kerria, bachelor's-button kerria, Japanese rose)

Even in deep shade, kerrias form dense round bushes; their yellow to orange spring flowers are more lavish, however, if the plants have some spring sunlight or are in the open shade of high-branched deciduous trees. In fall, their glossy coarsely toothed leaves, 1½ to 4 inches long, turn yellow; in winter the bare green stems provide color.

Variegated kerria, a dwarf variety, usually reaches 3 to 5 feet tall; its five-petaled yellow flowers, 1½ inches wide, last only a week. Globeflower kerria, a hardy hybrid, grows 5 to 7 feet tall and bears bright orange-yellow ball-shaped flowers 2 inches wide; they hang from the branches for two to three weeks. Both types sometimes produce a few flowers through summer and early fall. Their adaptability to varying degrees of shade makes them useful in many settings, from walled gardens and foundation plantings to wooded borders.

HOW TO GROW. Kerrias are hardy in Zones 5-9 but should be shielded from the wind. They adapt to almost any soil, doing best in moist, well-drained soil supplemented with 1 part of leaf mold or peat moss to every 2 parts of soil. To prevent soil from drying, mulch with a permanent 3- to 4-inch layer of wood chips, ground bark or chunky peat moss.

In Zones 5 and 6, prune winter-killed branch tips in the spring. All other pruning is done just after flowers fade because flower buds for the following year develop on the current year's growth. To rejuvenate plants, cut back older stems to the ground in early spring. Propagate new plants from cuttings of new growth taken in late spring or early summer. Plants can also be started by cutting off and replanting rooted underground offshoots.

L

LADY FERN See *Athyrium*
LADY'S SLIPPER See *Cypripedium*
LAUREL, MOUNTAIN See *Kalmia*
LAWN LEAF See *Dichondra*
LEATHER BERGENIA See *Bergenia*
LEATHERY POLYPODY See *Polypodium*
LEBANON SQUILL See *Puschkinia*

LEUCOJUM
L. vernum (spring snowflake); *L. aestivum* (summer snowflake, giant snowflake); *L. autumnale* (autumn snowflake)

The dainty snowflakes, with their green-tipped white flowers, are woodland plants that adapt easily to open shade in the cultivated garden. These small hardy bulbs can be massed under lightly foliaged trees or along fences or walls where they will receive early morning or late afternoon sun. They also look well among ferns and wildflowers or by streams and brooks. The spring snowflake grows 1 foot tall and has glossy green leaves. Its fragrant flowers, ¾ inch long, are borne singly on slender stems. In northwestern gardens, it blooms in late winter; in the eastern United States somewhat later. Summer snowflake's common name does not necessarily fit its blooming season; in the warmer regions of the West, summer snowflake blooms in the late autumn and winter, and on the Atlantic coast, it blooms in the spring and early summer. It, too, grows 1 foot tall, but it produces three to five nodding, bell-shaped flowers, ¾ inch long, on every

GLOBEFLOWER KERRIA
Kerria japonica 'Pleniflora'

SPRING SNOWFLAKE
Leucojum vernum

For climate zones and frost dates, see maps, pages 152-153.

DROOPING LEUCOTHOË
Leucothoë fontanesiana

MARTAGON LILY
Lilium martagon

NANKEEN LILY
Lilium testaceum

stem. Autumn snowflake is smaller and more fragile than the other two species, attaining a height of only 6 to 9 inches. Its tiny pink-tinged flowers usually appear in pairs and open in early fall.

HOW TO GROW. Spring snowflakes are hardy in Zones 4-8, summer snowflakes in Zones 4-9, autumn snowflakes in Zones 5-9. All three species do best in a light, sandy soil, but for summer snowflake the soil should be kept somewhat moist, while spring and autumn snowflakes require quick drainage. Plant snowflake bulbs in fall, setting them 3 to 4 inches deep and 4 inches apart. They may take a year or two to bloom. Snowflakes may be propagated in almost any season, even when growing, by lifting and dividing the bulbs, but they should remain out of the ground as brief a time as possible. Most gardeners prefer to acquire new plants by buying additional bulbs; they are quite inexpensive. Snowflakes also seed themselves, but they take three or four years to reach flowering size.

LEUCOTHOË

L. fontanesiana (drooping leucothoë, fetterbush)

A small shrub with arching branches and cascading sprays of fragrant white spring-blooming flowers, the drooping leucothoë grows in open to deep shade, but in low light it will have fewer flowers. The foliage of this broad-leaved evergreen changes color with the season: its leathery oval leaves, 4 to 7 inches long, are bronze-green when young, glossy deep green in summer and reddish-bronze in autumn and winter. At the northern edge of its hardiness range, it may lose some of its upper leaves during cold winters. The waxy white flowers, which appear in late spring, resemble lilies of the valley and hang in 2- to 3-inch clusters along the undersides of the branches. In five years, drooping leucothoë grows 3 to 5 feet high and spreads slowly by underground roots. It is useful on shaded slopes and combines well with mountain laurel, Oregon holly grape or Japanese skimmia in woodland settings. It tolerates city conditions as a border for patios or under deciduous or evergreen trees.

HOW TO GROW. Drooping leucothoë is hardy in Zones 5-9 and does best in a moist, acid, humus-rich soil. Plant it in the spring in Zones 5 and 6; from Zone 7 south, it can be set in the ground in either spring or fall. Space plants 4 feet apart, and to speed growth and encourage bushiness, scatter cottonseed meal or a fertilizer prepared for acid-loving plants under the shrubs in early spring. Prune out older canes back to the ground in very early spring to keep a plant in vigorous condition. Propagate from stem cuttings of new growth taken in summer or early fall; place them in moist sand and peat moss until the cuttings develop roots. Protect young plants with a mulch of leaves or wood chips during their first year.

LILIUM

L. canadense (Canada lily, wild yellow lily, meadow lily, yellow bell lily); *L. martagon* (martagon lily, Turk's-cap lily, turban lily); *L. superbum* (American Turk's-cap lily); *L. testaceum* (Nankeen lily); *L. tigrinum,* also called *L. lancifolium* (tiger lily)

All but one of these lilies, the Nankeen, are natural woodland plants—and the Nankeen, a hybrid, has a woodland lily in its ancestry. Thus all of them will produce abundant, bright-colored flowers in open or intermittent shade. These are tall lilies, some of them reaching a height of 8 feet, and their colors range from light yellow to deep salmon-red. They are outstanding when set in front of evergreens or against walls or fences, and are most effective planted in groups of three or more. The Nankeen lily also adapts to container culture and may be used as a pot plant on a shaded terrace as long as it has direct sunlight during some part of the day. These lilies should not be planted amid pachysandra or other heavy ground covers so thick they take moisture from the lily roots.

The Canada lily grows 2 to 6 feet tall, its leafy stalks bearing as many as 20 backward-curving flowers, each 2 to 3 inches across; these are pale yellow to orange-red with purple-brown spots and bloom in late June and July. The martagon lily grows 3 to 6 feet high, each plant producing as many as 15 to 25 or more backswept flowers, 2 to 3 inches across, in June and July; the flowers have an unpleasant smell. They come in a wide range of colors, depending on the variety. The American Turk's-cap lily, taller than the other lilies, reaches a height of 3 to 8 feet, and produces orange-scarlet flowers with brown spots and backswept petals from late July to early September; the flowers are 3 to 4 inches wide. The Nankeen lily can become 7 feet high and blooms in midsummer; its fragrant apricot or yellow back-curved flowers are often tinged with pink and are 3 inches wide. The tiger lily may grow 2 to 6 feet tall. It blooms in July and August, producing orange or salmon-red blooms with purple-black spots; these may be 3 to 5 inches across.

HOW TO GROW. Woodland lilies grow in Zones 4-10 and do best in a light, moist, well-drained sandy soil with leaf mold added to a depth of 1 foot. The soil may be neutral or slightly acid, but good drainage is important; lily roots should not be constantly wet. A 3-inch mulch of porous leaf mold or pine needles will help to keep the roots evenly moist year round and cool during the summer.

Plant lily bulbs in the fall or early spring, setting them 9 to 18 inches apart, and put a handful of gravel or sand under each one to improve drainage. Cover with 4 to 6 inches of soil, except for tiger lilies which grow best with a lighter covering of only 2 to 3 inches. Fertilize in early spring and again two months later to encourage flowering; use a standard garden fertilizer such as 5-10-5. In the warmer Zones 9 and 10, dig the bulbs after they have finished flowering and refrigerate them for eight weeks to give them their necessary dormancy period. Propagate additional lilies from the small bulblets surrounding the larger ones; these reach flowering age in two or three years.

LILY See *Lilium*
LILY, CANADA See *Lilium*
LILY, FAWN See *Erythronium*
LILY, MARTAGON See *Lilium*
LILY, NANKEEN See *Lilium*
LILY, TIGER See *Lilium*
LILY, TOAD See *Tricyrtis*
LILY, TROUT See *Erythronium*
LILY, TURK'S-CAP See *Lilium*
LILY OF THE VALLEY See *Convallaria*
LILY-OF-THE-VALLEY BUSH See *Pieris*
LILY-TURF See *Ophiopogon*

LOBELIA
L. cardinalis (cardinal flower); *L. erinus* (edging lobelia)

Although very different in size and habit of growth, both of these lobelias do well in open shade; in hot climates they may actually prefer a shaded site to a sunny one, since both are plants that need abundant moisture. Cardinal flower grows 1 to 4 feet tall and bears both leaves and flowers along a single stem. The leaves are about 4 inches long, pointed and narrow with serrated edges; they are sometimes bronze-green in color. The flowers appear from midsummer until

CARDINAL FLOWER
Lobelia cardinalis

For climate zones and frost dates, see maps, pages 152-153.

fall, in terminal clusters on foot-long spikes. The individual flowers are tubular in shape, opening into narrow lobes; generally they are bright red in color, although a few varieties are white or pink. In its wild form the cardinal flower is a perennial swamp flower, and in shade gardens it is often used along streams or wherever the soil is very moist.

Edging lobelia seldom grows more than 6 inches high, and the cultivated varieties come in two forms: trailing and mounded. The trailing variety is often used as a ground cover or in window boxes and hanging containers, while the mounding type is an excellent edging plant. Both are treated as annuals but may live over winter if protected by mulch. In their hybridized form they flower most profusely. They bloom through the summer and into fall, bearing flowers ½ to ¾ inch wide along their stems; usually they are a shade of blue but there are also white, pink and vivid red varieties. The leaves are ½ to 1 inch long with serrated edges.

HOW TO GROW. Cardinal flower, hardy in Zones 3-10, will thrive only in very moist soil enriched with compost. It may be started from seeds sown in the spring or fall. Under optimum conditions, cardinal flower will seed itself and spread naturally.

Edging lobelia grows in Zones 3-10 wherever the soil is rich and evenly moist. Because it takes eight weeks to reach flowering size, seeds are usually started indoors 10 to 12 weeks before the last frost is due. Provide 70° bottom heat and do not cover the seeds, as they are very small. Plants may also be purchased from nurseries. Set them in the ground 4 to 6 inches apart when all danger of frost is past. Following the first main period of bloom, plants should be sheared back to half their height to encourage more flowers. Fertilize monthly with a general-purpose fertilizer.

LOBULARIA

L. maritima, also called *Alyssum maritimum* (sweet alyssum)

Long a staple annual for gardens in full sun, sweet alyssum's flower colors—rose-pink, lavender and purple—are intensified by open shade. White varieties also do well in these conditions. Sweet alyssum is an easy-to-grow annual, quick to bloom, and has the added bonus of a honey-like fragrance. The normal species grows 10 inches high and is relatively open. Selected varieties grow only 3 to 4 inches high and form dense, spreading mounds of foliage. Their leaves are small, long and narrow; the tiny flowers bloom in clusters from early summer until frost. Among the recommended white varieties are Tiny Tim, Carpet of Snow, Snow Cloth Select and Little Gem. Rose-pink varieties include Rosie O'Day, rose-pink in cool weather, lavender-pink in hotter temperatures; and Wonderland, a darker rose-pink. In the blue-violet range, Royal Carpet has violet-colored flowers, while Violet Queen and Oriental Night are a deeper purple; in all three the clusters shade from lighter near the center to deeper at the edge. Navy Blue, another deep purple variety, has a less pronounced center area of lighter flowers. Sweet alyssum is an excellent low edging plant and also looks well in broad bands or drifts. It can be used as a ground cover around shrubs, perennials and other annuals, and as a temporary cover on slopes. Other uses include rock gardens, window boxes and hanging containers.

HOW TO GROW. Sweet alyssum does best in a well-drained slightly acid soil, although it tolerates a wide range of soils. Start it from nursery-grown plants, or from seeds sown directly into the garden as soon as the soil can be worked; from seed to flower takes six weeks. Seeds may also be started indoors four to six weeks before the last frost is due. Set sweet alyssum plants into the garden after all danger of frost

SWEET ALYSSUM
Lobularia maritima

is past, spacing them 6 to 8 inches apart; keep a good ball of soil around the roots so growth is not interrupted. In Zones 9 and 10, sweet alyssum will bloom the year round.

LONICERA

L. japonica 'Halliana' (Hall's Japanese honeysuckle); *L. sempervirens* (trumpet honeysuckle)

While their twining stems will ramble or climb in search of light, both of these honeysuckles are easy to grow in open shade, and their roots should actually be in deep shade. If the plant is trained on a trellis or a wall, the roots can be mulched. As a ground cover, it will shade its own roots. Both vines are evergreen in mild climates and are prized for their long-blooming flowers, dense foliage and rapid growth.

Japanese honeysuckle may grow 15 feet a year and reach a height of 30 feet; it can become a nuisance, shrouding everything in its path if not kept pruned. The tubular white flowers, 1½ inches long, bloom in pairs throughout the summer, turning yellow as they age, and are followed in the fall by black berries. The profuse foliage is oval or oblong, 1½ to 3½ inches long; in colder climates it turns bronze in fall.

Climbing up to 10 feet a year, trumpet honeysuckle may reach a maximum height of 50 feet. It blooms through most of the summer, bearing terminal clusters of orange to scarlet trumpet-shaped flowers, 2 inches long, that are yellow inside; in the fall these are followed by scarlet berries. The leaves are oval, 2 to 3 inches long, with downy, silvery undersurfaces. On each branch, the last one or two pairs of leaves are joined, forming a circle of foliage that the vine seems to pierce. In colder climates the foliage turns yellow in the fall.

HOW TO GROW. Japanese honeysuckle is hardy in Zones 6-9; trumpet honeysuckle in Zones 5-9. Both grow well in any moist, well-drained garden soil. Plant climbing honeysuckles 4 feet apart; as a ground cover Japanese honeysuckle can be planted 6 feet apart because it grows so vigorously. If necessary, keep roots cool with a 4-inch mulch of pine needles or shredded bark. Each spring scatter a layer of compost at the base of the plants. Prune in the fall after flowering ends; for Japanese honeysuckle this pruning and thinning should be severe to contain growth; trumpet honeysuckle needs only light pruning. Remove dead branches at this time. Honeysuckle branches take root where they touch the ground. But new plants may also be started with cuttings taken in mid- to late summer and rooted in peat moss and sand.

LYSIMACHIA

L. nummularia (moneywort, creeping Jenny, creeping Charlie)

Whatever the degree of shade, moneywort will rapidly spread across the ground to form a ruffled carpet 1 to 2 inches deep. Its creeping stems root so quickly that it may become a troublesome weed if not kept in check by pruning. But moneywort has the advantage of thriving in wet ground and deep shade where few other plants survive. Its 1-inch-round leaves remain bright green well into December in cold areas and are evergreen everywhere else. Masses of tiny yellow flowers, an inch or less across, bloom along the stems throughout the summer. On one variety, Aurea, the leaves are also yellow. This perennial is excellent for planting beside streams and pools or over wet banks. It can even stand occasional trampling when tucked around paving stones.

HOW TO GROW. Moneywort is hardy in Zones 4-10. It does well in moist, even soggy soil but adapts equally well to drier ground. Set out plants 12 to 18 inches apart at any time from the last frost of spring to the first frost of fall. Propagate by dividing established plants in spring or fall.

HALL'S JAPANESE HONEYSUCKLE
Lonicera japonica 'Halliana'

MONEYWORT
Lysimachia nummularia

For climate zones and frost dates, see maps, pages 152-153.

CREEPING MAHONIA
Mahonia repens

VIRGINIA BLUEBELL
Mertensia virginica

M

MAHONIA

M. aquifolium; M. nervosa; M. repens (creeping mahonia)
(all called Oregon holly grape)

The Oregon holly grapes, native to the mountains of the Pacific northwest, are broad-leaved evergreens that do well in open shade and are especially hardy. Though related to neither hollies nor grapes, their shiny spiked leaves resemble the first and their blue-black berries the second. All of them bloom in spring, producing erect clusters of fragrant yellow flowers at the ends of the stems. In cold areas the foliage of the Oregon holly grapes turns a handsome purple-bronze. Depending on their size, these three species are used for foundation plantings, rock gardens or open woodland settings, and *M. repens* makes a colorful ground cover.

M. aquifolium grows 3 to 5 feet tall and has prickly stalks and spiny, polished leaves composed of five to nine leaflets, 3 inches long. The flower clusters are 3 inches high. *M. nervosa* grows only 2 feet high. Its spiny leaves are composed of three to ten leaflets, narrower than those of aquifolium but just as long, and its flower clusters are 8 inches high. *M. repens* seldom becomes more than 12 inches high and spreads rapidly on underground stems. Its leaves consist of three to seven leaflets, each 1½ to 2½ inches long, and its flower clusters are 3 inches high. The fruit is almost black.

HOW TO GROW. Oregon holly grapes are hardy in Zones 5-10 and do well in any moist, well-drained, acid soil. *M. nervosa* is the least hardy of these three species. Plant them in the spring or early fall, setting taller species 3 feet apart, ground covers 12 inches apart. In northern zones place them in a sheltered location to prevent winter winds from drying out their foliage. Mulch plants with 2 to 3 inches of pine needles or well-rotted oak leaves to prevent loss of moisture, and renew this mulch as needed. Fertilize Oregon holly grapes in the early spring with cottonseed meal or a fertilizer prepared for acid-loving plants, dusted around the base of the plant. To shape plants or to control their size, prune out the tallest canes in the early spring. Propagate holly grapes by removing and replanting suckers.

MAPLE See *Acer*
MAY APPLE See *Podophyllum*

MERTENSIA

M. virginica (Virginia bluebell)

A sturdy spring-blooming perennial, the Virginia bluebell favors medium to open shade and is often used in moist woodland settings. Its inch-long trumpet-shaped blooms form nodding clusters atop 1- to 2-foot stems. Buds and newly opened flowers are pink, but the flowers turn blue as they mature. A variety, *M. virginica alba,* has white flowers, and there is also a variety, *M. virginica rubra,* whose flowers remain pink. The foliage, which emerges as pink shoots, matures into silvery green leaves 3 to 7 inches long. These die back in midsummer, so ferns are often planted with Virginia bluebells to fill in the empty spots. Bees seek out Virginia bluebells for their nectar.

HOW TO GROW. Virginia bluebells are hardy in Zones 4-8 and do well in a humus-rich acid soil. Keep the soil moist in spring, although in summer, when the plants become dormant, the soil may be allowed to become slightly dry. Plant root segments anytime from early summer until the ground freezes, setting them 1½ feet apart and deep enough so their tops are 1 inch below the surface. They may also be started from seed sown in spring, summer or fall; seedlings will flower in three years.

MIMULUS
M. hybridus; M. cupreus (both called monkey flower)

These two forms of the monkey flower, like the woodland wildflowers that supply their parentage, do well in any area of open shade. Their brightly colored spotted, dotted and streaked flowers derive their common name from their resemblance to monkey faces. Their tubular flaring blooms, 2 inches across, are borne, several at a time, on 8-inch to 2-foot spikes that rise above 6- to 12-inch mounds of toothed-edged foliage. The flowers bloom from early summer until frost and come in variegated colors that may combine red, yellow, white, gold, brown or maroon. Although technically perennials, they are warm-climate plants and are usually grown outdoors in temperate zones as annuals. In the shade garden they are useful in borders.

HOW TO GROW. Monkey flowers do best in cool, moist soils and will even tolerate wet soils. Buy nursery-grown plants and set them in the ground in the spring, when all danger of frost is past, spacing them 6 inches apart. Or start plants from seed indoors 10 to 12 weeks before the last frost is due, keeping the soil temperature at 70° to 75° until the seeds germinate. The seedlings may be transplanted directly into the garden, or they may be planted in 8-inch pots and plunged into the ground—to be lifted in the fall and brought indoors for winter bloom. Feed monkey flowers monthly during the summer with an all-purpose garden fertilizer and mulch, if necessary, to keep the soil cool and damp.

MOCCASIN FLOWER See *Cypripedium*
MONDO GRASS See *Ophiopogon*
MONEYWORT See *Lysimachia*
MONKEY FLOWER See *Mimulus*
MOTHER FERN See *Asplenium*
MOUNTAIN LAUREL See *Kalmia*

MUSCARI
M. armeniacum (Armenian grape hyacinth); *M.* 'Blue Spike'; *M. botryoides album* (common white grape hyacinth); *M. comosum* 'Plumosum' (feather hyacinth); *M. tubergenianum,* also called *M. aucheri tubergenianum* (tubergen grape hyacinth)

Resembling small upside-down bunches of grapes and having a faint grapelike aroma, the blooms of grape hyacinths form a spring carpet under high-branching deciduous trees. The grape hyacinth's tiny, clustered flowers are pitcher- or globe-shaped, like those of the true hyacinth but much smaller. Though the flowers disappear after blooming, their place is marked for the following year by winter-hardy grasslike foliage, 6 to 8 inches long, which appears in the fall.

The Armenian grape hyacinth grows to 9 inches tall with bright blue flowers in tight clusters on 4- to 8-inch stalks. A variety, Blue Spike, is notable for its clusters of double flowers carried on single stalks. The common white grape hyacinth grows 6 to 12 inches high and bears globe-shaped white flowers in tightly packed bunches of 12 to 20 on a single stalk. The reddish-purple flowers of the feather hyacinth are divided into fine shreds; they are borne in clusters of 50 or more on 10- to 14-inch stems. The tubergen grape hyacinth has pale blue bells on the top of its 8-inch stem, with darker blue bells beneath.

Grape hyacinths adapt easily and look natural in borders and rock gardens under shrubs and trees with light foliage.

HOW TO GROW. Grape hyacinths are hardy in Zones 3-9 and do well in any well-drained garden soil. Plant the bulbs in late summer or early fall, setting them 3 inches deep and 3 inches apart. No special care is necessary. The bulbs may

MONKEY FLOWER
TOP: *Mimulus hybridus;* BOTTOM: *M. cupreus*

GRAPE HYACINTH
Muscari tubergenianum

For climate zones and frost dates, see maps, pages 152-153.

WOODLAND FORGET-ME-NOT
Myosotis sylvatica

BABY-BLUE-EYES
Nemophila menziesii

be dug up and divided in midsummer for additional plantings elsewhere, but they are so inexpensive that it is easier just to buy more. Grape hyacinths also seed themselves, taking three years to reach the blooming stage.

MYOSOTIS
M. sylvatica, also called *M. oblongata* (woodland forget-me-not)

As much a part of the spring garden as tulips and daffodils, forget-me-nots bloom in both open and medium shade and to some extent even in deep shade. The sky-blue yellow-centered flowers are only ¼ inch across and are borne in graceful clusters at the ends of slender stems from early spring to early summer. The plants themselves, growing in loose mounds or ball-shaped clumps, are 6 to 24 inches tall, depending on the variety. The hairy leaves are long and narrow. Many varieties are available, produced under cultivation, and varieties of two other species, *M. alpestris* and *M. dissitiflora,* are often confused with woodland forget-me-nots. Some of the true varieties include Alba, with white flowers; Compacta, dense and low-growing; Fischeri, low-growing, with blue-pink flowers; Oblongata Perfecta, early blooming with large blue flowers; Robusta Grandiflora, also with larger flowers; Rosea, with pink-rose flowers; Stricta, with more erect growth; Blue Ball, with very compact, 6-inch ball-like growth; and Ultramarine, with dark blue flowers. Forget-me-nots are used in beds and borders, as edgings, in rock gardens and in combination with spring bulbs.

HOW TO GROW. Forget-me-nots need an evenly moist soil enriched with compost or peat moss, and do best in areas where summer temperatures are cool. You can easily start plants from seed. For earliest spring bloom, sow the seeds outdoors in late summer or fall; in Zones 3-8, plants started in the fall have to be wintered over in cold frames. Or sow seeds outdoors in spring as soon as the ground can be worked for bloom from late spring until midsummer. Once established, forget-me-nots readily seed themselves and come up and bloom year after year.

MYRTLE, CREEPING See *Vinca*

N

NEMOPHILA
N. menziesii (baby-blue-eyes)

One of the few plants to produce truly blue flowers, baby-blue-eyes does best in areas of open shade, where it gets good light but no sun, or in areas of intermittent shade where the afternoon sun is blocked. In fact, the natural occurrence of baby-blue-eyes in shady areas has given rise to its botanical name, coming from the Greek words *nemos,* or grove, and *phileo,* to love. A fast-growing annual, it sends out trailing, succulent stems that spread up to 12 inches wide and grow to a height of 6 to 10 inches. The foliage is finely divided and fernlike, 2 inches in length. Each flower, borne on a short, delicate stem, has five rounded petals that form an open cup 1 to 1½ inches across. The flowers are sky blue with white centers and open all summer long; at night they are fragrant. Varieties of baby-blue-eyes include Alba, with white flowers; Crambeoides, with light-blue flowers veined in purple; Marginata, with blue flowers edged in white; Grandiflora, with larger flowers; *N. menziesii atomaria,* with white flowers dotted with purple; and *N. menziesii discoidalis,* with brown-purple flowers edged in white. Baby-blue-eyes can be used in the rock garden or flower border, planted in drifts or as an edging. They are especially attractive when grown as a ground cover with spring-flowering bulbs. They can also be planted as trailing plants in window boxes or hanging baskets. In bouquets, the flowers last two to three days.

HOW TO GROW. Baby-blue-eyes does well in any light, moist, well-drained garden soil. For best growth, it needs summers with cool, moist evenings, like those of the northern California coast, where it is native. As plants are difficult to transplant, they should be started from seeds sown directly into the garden as soon as soil can be worked in the spring. Scatter seeds thickly, then thin seedlings to stand 6 inches apart. Feed monthly during the summer with an all-purpose garden fertilizer, and mulch, if necessary, to keep soil moist and cool. In frost-free areas of Zones 9 and 10, seeds may be sown in the fall for flowers in winter and early spring.

NICOTIANA
N. alata 'Grandiflora,' also called *N. affinis; N. alata* 'Nicki Red' (both called flowering tobacco)

In open shade along the north side of a house or in intermittent shade where it gets some sunlight each day, annual flowering tobacco provides masses of color and a heavy, pleasant fragrance. The velvety leaves have a narcotic effect and should not be put in the mouth; they grow up to 4 inches long and form ground-hugging clumps. The flower stalks rise above them to a height of 1 to 4 feet, depending on the variety; newer hybrids usually grow no more than 1½ feet tall. The flowers open in loose clusters at the top of the stalk from midsummer until frost. Each flower has a long tube that flares out into a trumpet shape. Colors range from white to scarlet, wine, rose, salmon, crimson, cream, chartreuse, lavender, mauve, maroon and chocolate.

In older varieties, flowering tobacco would open its blooms only after dusk; more recent varieties keep their flowers open day and night. Nicki Red is one of a group of hybrids that produces an exceptional number of flowers on many-branched plants 18 to 24 inches tall; it is a rich crimson-red. Other colors in the same group are white, pink, rose, red, lime and deep rose. There are also compact varieties less than 12 inches tall, among them Sensation and Dwarf Potpourri, both mixtures of colors; Crimson King, Crimson Bedder, White Bedder and Lime Sherbet. All the flowering tobaccos are useful for mass plantings in beds or for growing in tubs. They are effective when used as a vertical accent among annuals that are trailing in habit.

HOW TO GROW. Flowering tobacco does well in any moist, well-drained garden soil. It may be started from purchased plants or from seeds, but as seeds are very small it is best to start them indoors four to six weeks before the last frost is due. Do not cover them, as they need light to germinate, and provide bottom heat of 75°. When all frost danger is past, set plants into the garden, spacing them 9 to 12 inches apart. Plants begin to bloom six weeks after seeds are sown. Feed with an all-purpose garden fertilizer monthly during the summer, and mulch in hot weather to help maintain soil moisture. If allowed to go to seed, flowering tobacco will continue producing plants year after year. In Zones 9 and 10, the plants often survive more than one season.

OLD-MAN'S BEARD See *Chionanthus*

ONOCLEA
O. sensibilis (sensitive fern, bead fern)

The sensitive fern grows in medium shade and, if watered frequently, in open or intermittent shade. It rises to a height of 2 to 4 feet and spreads rapidly on underground stems, or rhizomes, forming a dense mass of foliage that makes it

FLOWERING TOBACCO
Nicotiana alata 'Nicki Red'

SENSITIVE FERN
Onoclea sensibilis

For climate zones and frost dates, see maps, pages 152-153.

DWARF LILY-TURF
Ophiopogon japonicus

ROYAL FERN
Osmunda regalis

useful as a ground cover or background planting. Its foliage appears in two stages: in spring the light-green sterile fronds unfurl, the coarsely toothed but delicate leaflets seeming almost to have been cut out with scissors. These fronds are triangular, 2 to 4 feet long, and sensitive to frost; in fall they turn brown and die. The fertile fronds rise in late summer on erect stalks 1 to 2 feet tall; their leaflets curl so tightly around their spore clusters that they resemble green beads. These beads turn brown and remain on the plant until the following spring when they burst open to spread the spores.

HOW TO GROW. The sensitive fern is hardy in Zones 4-8 and the northern part of Zone 9. It does best in slightly acid to neutral soil composed of 1 part loam, 1 part sand and 2 parts leaf mold or peat moss. The soil should be constantly moist, even boggy. A mulch of leaves or evergreen boughs will help retain moisture and provide winter protection.

Plant rhizomes in spring or fall, setting them 1 inch deep and 2 feet apart. Fertilize in spring by spreading bone meal at the base of the ferns in the proportion of 1 ounce per square yard, or use fish emulsion fertilizer diluted to half the strength recommended on the label. Remove dead fronds in late spring after spore clusters have opened; propagate in spring from spores collected immediately after the bead clusters burst open or by dividing the roots in spring or fall.

OPHIOPOGON

O. japonicus (dwarf lily-turf, mondo grass)

Dwarf lily-turf, a grasslike evergreen ground cover, thrives in medium to open shade, its arching leaves, 8 to 12 inches long, forming mounds 4 to 6 inches tall. In early summer, tiny white or lavender blooms less than ¼ inch wide appear on short 2- to 3-inch flower stalks. These are followed by clusters of ¼-inch blue berries. A variegated form, Striatus, has white-striped leaves; a diminutive form, Compacta, is only 2 inches in height. Dwarf lily-turf grows slowly at first, creeping on fleshy underground stems, but eventually its rate of growth quickens. It is a useful plant under trees and shrubs with open foliage, requiring little care.

HOW TO GROW. Dwarf lily-turf is hardy in Zones 8-10 and does best in a moist, rich soil supplemented with leaf mold or peat moss. In the northernmost limits of its growing area, it should have a location with some protection from the wind, to prevent winter damage to its foliage. Set out plants in spring, spacing them 6 to 12 inches apart. Propagate by dividing established plants in early spring.

OSMUNDA

O. cinnamomea (cinnamon fern); *O. claytoniana* (interrupted fern); *O. regalis* (royal fern)

The tall osmundas are among the most adaptable of ferns, thriving equally well in any amount of shade, from open to deep. These 4- to 6-foot-tall perennials spread very slowly along masses of thick woody underground stems, or rhizomes. When shredded, this root system becomes the osmunda fiber used as a growing medium for orchids and other plants with aerial roots. The osmundas are often found growing wild in marshy areas, and in shade gardens they are used along the banks of ponds or brooks or in moist borders as a background for smaller plants or as single specimens.

The cinnamon fern sends up hairy white leaf buds called fiddleheads in early spring; these open into fertile fronds 1 to 2 feet long, which are covered with round spore clusters that are at first green, then cinnamon brown. The leaflets of these fronds hug the stalks so closely that the fronds resemble wooden sticks. When the spores have burst their casings, the leaflets wither and fall to the ground. Later in spring the sterile fronds appear, lance-shaped and 2 to 5 feet long, with pairs of coarsely toothed leaflets 8 inches wide, pointed and tufted with brown woolly hairs where they join the stalks. These remain green until killed by winter frost.

The white, furry leaf buds of the interrupted fern closely resemble those of the cinnamon fern, but when the 4-foot-fronds unfurl, their reproductive arrangements are different. At the perimeter of the plant, all the fronds are sterile and remain green until the first frost. Inside, the fronds contain both sterile and fertile leaflets. The latter are located in the middle of each frond and consist of two to five pairs of spore-bearing leaflets 2 to 3 inches long among pairs of sterile leaflets 6 to 8 inches long. After discharging their spores in early summer, the fertile leaflets fall off, leaving the center of the frond bare—"interrupted."

The royal fern is one of the largest native American ferns, 6 feet tall. Its fronds are not lacy, but look more like the foliage of a locust tree, with widely spaced pointed oval leaflets borne on branching stems. The leaflets are red when they open, turning green as they mature, and are 4 inches long. The fertile leaflets, at the tip of each frond, contain hundreds of bright green spore clusters, covering the stem so densely that they resemble clusters of tiny flowers. After scattering their spores, the fertile leaflets turn brown, falling off at the first frost.

HOW TO GROW. Osmunda ferns are hardy in Zones 3-8, and the royal fern will also survive in Zones 9 and 10 if it is kept constantly wet. They do best in slightly acid soil composed of 1 part garden loam, 1 part coarse sand and 2 parts leaf mold or peat moss. The soil should be constantly wet for the cinnamon fern and royal fern; constantly moist for the interrupted fern. A mulch of leaves or evergreen boughs will help retain moisture while protecting the roots during winter.

Plant osmunda rhizomes in the spring or fall, setting them 1 inch deep and 3 inches apart. Fertilize in spring by spreading bone meal at the base of the ferns at the rate of 1 ounce per square yard; or use fish emulsion fertilizer diluted to half the strength recommended. Remove dead fronds in fall; the fertile top fronds of royal fern may also be cut back at this time. Osmundas spread slowly in an ever-widening circle, and as they do the center of the clump dies. This area may be filled with new ferns, propagated by sowing spores collected right after the spore clusters burst in early summer or by dividing crowns in spring before new growth appears.

OXYDENDRUM

O. arboreum (sorrel tree, sourwood)

A small summer-flowering tree with vivid fall foliage, the sorrel grows well in open or dappled shade, although for the most flowers and the brightest autumn color, it needs sun during some part of the day. This slow-growing tree seldom exceeds a height of 20 feet and width of 10 to 15 feet. Its single or multiple trunks have drooping lower branches that sometimes dip to the ground. The glossy 4- to 8-inch-long leaves are tinged with red when they first unfurl in spring, changing to dark green in summer and to brilliant scarlet in the fall. In midsummer, tiny fragrant white bell-shaped flowers dangle in clusters 6 to 8 inches long at the ends of branches. They resemble miniature lilies of the valley and are followed in fall by 6- to 10-inch gray-green seed pods in hanging finger-like clusters. Sorrel is useful planted alone or combined with taller trees and such shrubs as rhododendrons and azaleas that require the same growing conditions.

HOW TO GROW. The sorrel tree is hardy in Zones 5-8 and thrives in a moist, well-drained acid soil. To improve drainage, add 1 part peat moss or leaf mold for every 2 parts of

SORREL TREE
Oxydendrum arboreum

For climate zones and frost dates, see maps, pages 152-153.

PACHYSANDRA
Pachysandra terminalis

WOODBINE
Parthenocissus quinquefolia

soil. Choose a location with some protection from the wind and plant young trees in early spring. Sorrel trees normally do not need fertilizing, but a weak tree may be strengthened by scattering cottonseed meal or an all-purpose fertilizer around its base in spring. Pruning is rarely required, but if necessary it should be done in late winter or early spring.

P

PACHISTIMA See *Paxistima*
PATIENT LUCY See *Impatiens*

PACHYSANDRA

P. terminalis (Japanese pachysandra, Japanese spurge)

As if made for the shade, Japanese pachysandra stays green and spreads rapidly even under maples, beeches and sycamores, whose shadows are deep and whose root systems are shallow and competitive. In difficult situations, it is likely to do better than almost anything else that could be tried. This evergreen ground cover grows best, however, in open, intermittent shade. It has innumerable uses: in foundation plantings along north-facing walls, spreading over large expanses of sloping ground, in borders and beds for city gardens shadowed by high buildings, in circular beds around the bases of trees. It is so aggressive, however, that it should not be planted where its roots will choke out bulbs or siphon off the moisture and nutrients needed by such broad-leaved evergreens as Japanese andromeda or leucothoë. It is sometimes necessary to cut and remove underground runners to prevent this vigorous ground cover from encroaching on adjacent plantings.

Japanese pachysandra grows from 6 to 8 inches high. Its leaves are 2 to 4 inches long, wedge-shaped to oval and toothed at the tips; they grow clustered and particularly dense at the tips of the stems, creating a neat, bushy carpet of foliage that stays green through severe winters. Above it bloom short spikes of tiny white flowers in spring; these are sometimes followed by inconspicuous white berries in the fall. A more prostrate variety, Green Carpet, grows closer to the ground, usually is a deeper green and flowers more abundantly; it forms a neat border for a walk or flower bed.

HOW TO GROW. Japanese pachysandra, hardy in Zones 5-8, grows best in rich, moist, acid soil. In dense or deep shade, enrich the soil with peat moss or well-rotted leaf mold. Set out plants in spring or early summer, placing them 6 to 12 inches apart; water them well to get them started. Conserve moisture with a mulch of wood chips or ground bark. If planted under trees with strong surface root systems, pachysandra will benefit from an occasional feeding with a high-nitrogen fertilizer. Under other deciduous trees and shrubs, the fallen leaves supply sufficient nourishment, besides serving as a mulch.

If the plants are attacked by euonymus scale, the pest can be controlled with dormant oil spray in winter. Propagate Japanese pachysandra by lifting and cutting sections of runners that contain several new plants or from rooted stem cuttings taken in early summer from new growth.

PARTHENOCISSUS

P. quinquefolia (woodbine, Virginia creeper)

The woodbine is a useful vine, growing vigorously in medium to open shade and in almost any soil. Its deciduous leaves turn brilliant crimson in the fall before they drop. It is a strong climber, reaching a possible height of 80 feet by means of sticky, twining tendrils that fasten to any rough surface. The dull green foliage, dark on top, pale green beneath, consists of five leaflets; each leaflet is 1½ to 4 inches long, with serrated edges and a pointed tip. In early summer, there are inconspicuous yellow-green flowers, followed by pea-sized blue-black berries. The woodbine's rampant foliage is best used to cover stone or brick walls, fences, trellises or arbors. For more confined areas, two useful varieties are Engelmannii, with smaller, more delicate leaves; and Saint-Paulii, which also has smaller leaves and clings more tenaciously to stone and brick.

HOW TO GROW. Woodbine is hardy in Zones 4-10 and does well in any moist, well-drained garden soil. Plant young vines in late fall or early spring, setting them 4 to 6 inches apart. Support young plants with canes or stakes; if grown against a high wall, young woodbine may need the support of vertical wires, spaced 2 feet apart. Pinch off growing tips to encourage branching. Water during dry spells. Feed each spring by sprinkling all-purpose fertilizer around the base of each plant. Prune and remove dead branches in early spring to control the vine's size; thin out again in summer if foliage becomes too dense. Propagate from stem cuttings of new growth taken in late summer or start new plants by fastening stems to the ground until they take root.

PAXISTIMA (PACHISTIMA)

P. canbyi, also called *Pachistima canbyi* (Canby pachistima, ratstripper)

Canby pachistima, a dwarf evergreen shrub that grows only 6 to 12 inches tall, flourishes in dappled to open shade. Its trailing branches, densely filled with ¼- to 1-inch leaves form a bright green mat in summer, changing to bronze in winter. Tiny, inconspicuous reddish-brown flowers bloom between the leaves in late spring. This creeping perennial spreads slowly. Its thick foliage is useful in front of azaleas and rhododendrons or for edging a flower bed; plants can be clipped to form low hedges.

HOW TO GROW. Canby pachistima is hardy in Zones 5-9; it will tolerate some sun in Zones 5-8 but must have shade in the hottest parts of Zone 9. Plant in moist, well-drained acid soil. Add 1 part of peat moss or leaf mold for every 2 parts of soil to improve drainage. Set out plants in spring, spacing them about 12 inches apart. Provide a permanent mulch, 3 to 4 inches deep, of wood chips, ground bark or chunky peat moss to maintain moisture and keep out weeds. Propagate new plants by dividing established ones in spring. Plants may also be started from stem cuttings taken in summer.

PERIWINKLE See *Vinca*

PHLOX

P. carolina, also called *P. suffruticosa* (Carolina phlox, thick-leaved phlox); *P. divaricata*, also called *P. canadensis* (wild sweet William, wild blue phlox); *P. stolonifera*, also called *P. reptans* (creeping phlox)

These three versions of one of the most widely grown garden perennials are woodland plants, especially recommended for open shade. Carolina phlox grows 2½ to 4 feet tall and has thick leaves up to 5 inches long. Its dense cone-shaped flower clusters, which are composed of hundreds of ¾-inch pink, purple or white flowers, bloom from late spring to midsummer, and if the spent flowers are snipped off, new blooms will usually appear in late summer or early fall. This variety, which is fragrant, is suitable for planting under high-branching trees or at the rear of shady flower beds. The other two varieties, which are low-growing, are widely used as ground covers or rock garden plants. Wild sweet William becomes 8 to 18 inches tall. Its loose clusters of fragrant blue flowers, up to 1½ inches wide, appear in late spring. Creep-

CANBY PACHISTIMA
Paxistima canbyi

WILD SWEET WILLIAM
Phlox divaricata

For climate zones and frost dates, see maps, pages 152-153.

JAPANESE ANDROMEDA
Pieris japonica

COMMON MAY APPLE
Podophyllum peltatum

ing phlox has trailing stems, 6 to 12 inches long, that root as they creep along the ground. It has leaves that are 1½ to 4 inches long and bears clusters of 1-inch pale purple, blue, pink or white flowers in spring.

HOW TO GROW. All of these phloxes are hardy in Zones 4-7 and may occasionally be grown as far north and south as Zones 3 and 9. They do best in a moist, well-drained soil composed of 1 part leaf mold or peat moss to every 2 parts of soil. Set out plants in early fall, spacing Carolina phlox about 18 inches apart, wild sweet William and creeping phlox 8 to 12 inches apart. Keep the ground moist, and water frequently in hot, dry weather. Thin out Carolina phlox every spring, removing all but four or five of the lowest-growing shoots in each clump. Remove faded flowers on all species and shear wild sweet William and creeping phlox halfway back to stimulate new foliage. Propagate all three species by taking stem cuttings in summer; rooted cuttings will flower the next year. Or divide clumps after flowers fade. Carolina phlox may be divided when plants are four to five years old, wild sweet William and creeping phlox when plants are two years old.

PIERIS

P. japonica (Japanese andromeda, lily-of-the-valley bush)

A broad-leaved evergreen shrub with year-round ornamental value, the Japanese andromeda grows to best advantage in intermittent shade; it needs some sunshine in the spring to promote the most lavish display of flowers. The plant grows 4 to 6 feet high, with a neat profile that seldom needs pruning. Its glossy leaves, 1½ to 3 inches long, are coppery bronze when young, turning dark green as they mature. Tight white buds for the following year's flowers form in 5-inch-long cascading clusters in the summer, decorate the plant through the fall and winter, and burst into bloom the next spring. The flowers, which resemble lilies of the valley, last four to five weeks.

Among the cultivated varieties of Japanese andromeda, the dwarf variety Bonsai and the slow-growing Compacta are especially useful for planting under trees or against house foundations. One variety, Dorothy Wyckoff, offers winter color in the form of dark red buds and bronze-green foliage, as well as long pale pink flower panicles in the spring. Variegata has white-margined leaves that give the shrub special value as an accent plant in the shade.

HOW TO GROW. Japanese andromeda is hardy in Zones 5-9. Plant it in acid soil, adding 1 part of peat moss or leaf mold for every 2 parts of soil to improve drainage. Choose a location with some protection from the wind to prevent winter damage to foliage. Keep the ground moist; if necessary provide a permanent mulch, 3 to 4 inches deep, of wood chips, ground bark or chunky peat moss. Normally Japanese andromeda does not need to be fertilized, but a weak plant may be strengthened by lightly scattering cottonseed meal on the ground below it in early spring. Faded flowers should be removed so the plant's energy will go into new growth rather than into seed production.

PINK SUMMER SWEET See *Clethra*

PODOPHYLLUM

P. peltatum (common May apple)

The common May apple, a wildflower in both coniferous and deciduous woodlands of the eastern United States, is at its best in open to deep shade. Growing 12 to 18 inches high, it unfurls its tightly rolled leaves only when it approaches full size, usually producing a pair of three- to seven-lobed leaves almost a foot wide. A hanging cup-shaped waxy white flower

1 to 2 inches wide opens in the fork between the two leaves. In midsummer the foliage dies and the flower matures into a 1- to 2-inch yellow fruit, which is poisonous, as are seeds and leaves. Common May apple spreads rapidly on thick, creeping underground stems, or rhizomes, to form large colonies that may overpower a small garden or weaker plants.

HOW TO GROW. Common May apple is hardy in Zones 3-10, doing best in a moist soil rich in leaf mold, with a moderate acidity. Plant rhizomes 1 to 1½ inches deep in the fall, with the tips pointing up. Or start plants from seed, removing them from the pulp as soon as the fruit ripens; plant the seeds immediately. Common May apples often seed themselves, and seedlings can be transplanted at any time. Additional plants may also be propagated by dividing established colonies in late summer or fall.

POLYPODIUM

P. aureum, also called *Phlebodium aureum* (rabbit's foot fern, golden polypody); *P. polycarpon grandiceps* (climbing bird's nest fern); *P. scouleri,* also called *Goniophlebium scouleri* (leathery polypody, leatherleaf); *P. vulgare* (common polypody, adder's fern, brakeroot, wall fern) (all called polypody)

The thick, furry stems of the polypodies creep along the surface of the ground, climbing over rocks and tree trunks. Small scars that develop where old fronds have broken off— the "footprints"—account for their Latin name. These perennial ferns with leathery foliage thrive in varying degrees of shade: open shade is best for rabbit's foot fern, medium shade for climbing bird's nest fern and leathery polypody, and medium to open or intermittent shade for common polypody. All but the common polypody are deciduous.

The rabbit's foot fern has a golden-brown stem as much as 1 inch in diameter. Its blue-green fronds are 3 feet or more long and 10 inches or more wide. Its pairs of deeply cut leaflets have wavy edges and pointed tips. The golden spore clusters on the leaves dust them with yellow powder when the fern is mature. The foliage lasts for many months but eventually turns yellow and withers.

The unusual fronds of the climbing bird's nest fern are 1 to 2 feet long, erect, thick and straplike for much of their length, but on some fronds the tips branch out to form crests 6 inches wide. The fronds grow 1 inch apart along a dense network of scaly green stems, and the plant's small spore clusters are scattered along the backs of the leaves. The leathery polypody has a white stem and deeply cut waxy triangular fronds 1 to 2 feet long. Its pairs of leaflets are 6 to 8 inches wide, rounded at the tips, and bear round spore clusters in rows paralleling the midvein on the undersides.

The common polypody, smallest of the group, has a scale-covered stem and produces a dense growth of narrow spear-shaped fronds, 6 to 12 inches long and 2 inches wide. Its pairs of leaflets are deeply cut, rounded at the tips, and lined on the undersides with two rows of large round spore clusters, greenish-white when young, golden- and reddish-brown when mature. The evergreen leaves curl up in winter and unfurl again in spring, becoming darker green as they age.

Polypody ferns can be grown in crevices of walls, in rock gardens or in woodland gardens. Common polypody's dense habit of growth also makes it useful as a ground cover.

HOW TO GROW. Rabbit's foot fern is hardy in Zones 9 and 10, climbing bird's nest fern in Zone 10, leathery polypody in Zones 5-10 and common polypody in the cooler climates of Zones 4-8. They all do best in a slightly acid soil composed of 1 part garden loam, 1 part coarse sand and 2 parts leaf mold or peat moss. The soil should be constantly moist but not

LEATHERY POLYPODY
Polypodium scouleri

COMMON POLYPODY
Polypodium vulgare

For climate zones and frost dates, see maps, pages 152-153.

SIEBOLD'S PRIMROSE
Primula sieboldii

STRIPED SQUILL
Puschkinia scilloides

soggy. A mulch of leaves or evergreen boughs will help retain moisture while protecting the roots of the common polypody during winter.

Plant polypodies in spring or fall, setting their roots 1 inch below the soil surface and 2 feet apart. Fertilize in spring by spreading bone meal at the base of the ferns at the rate of 1 ounce per square yard, or use fish emulsion fertilizer diluted to half the strength recommended. Remove dead fronds in fall or spring. Propagate by sowing spores collected in summer or fall or by dividing roots in spring or fall.

PRIMROSE See *Primula*

PRIMULA

P. juliae hybrids (Julia primrose); *P. sieboldii* (Siebold's primrose)

The intense colors of the flowers of perennial primroses brighten areas of open or dappled shade. Julia primrose may be used in rock gardens, planted among ferns or other non-smothering woodland plants, or massed under open spring-flowering trees such as redbud or dogwood. Siebold's primrose does best in bog gardens or along shaded brooks.

The many hybrids of Julia primrose tolerate warm temperatures and dryness better than most primroses. Their wrinkled, elongated oval leaves are 4 inches long. Tight clumps of evergreen foliage spread by means of underground stems, or stolons, and form a thick mat on the ground. In midspring the 1-inch flowers, on stems 2 inches high, hide the foliage. Colors range from white to cream, yellow, pink, scarlet, deep red, lilac and deep purple. Siebold's primrose has large crinkled oval leaves 4 to 8 inches long with scalloped edges. The foliage dies back after the plant blooms and reappears the following spring. Clusters of 1½-inch flowers are borne on 8- to 10-inch stems in midspring; colors include white, pink, rose, crimson or purple; cultivated varieties may have larger flowers or be fringed, bicolored or have white centers.

HOW TO GROW. Both Julia primrose and Siebold's primrose are hardy in Zones 5-8. Primroses are native to cool, moist climates and do best in acid soil supplemented with organic matter such as compost, leaf mold or peat moss. They should be watered deeply during dry periods. In early spring, dust with a fertilizer made for acid-loving plants. Use a mulch to keep soil cool in summer. In areas with freezing temperatures but little snow cover, plants benefit from the protection of evergreen boughs in winter. Propagate by sowing seeds in a cold frame as soon as they ripen so they are subjected to winter freezing and thawing. Divide plants immediately after they flower if they become overcrowded. When setting divisions into the garden, space them 6 to 12 inches apart. Primroses are seldom bothered by pests.

PUSCHKINIA

P. scilloides, also called *P. libanotica, P. sicula* (striped squill, Lebanon squill); *P. scilloides alba*

The small striped squill, similar in size to the smaller species of the bulb plant known simply as squill, does best in open or intermittent shade. Its tiny flowers cluster like hyacinths along the 3- to 6-inch stem and have a faint fragrance. The flowers of striped squill are white with blue stripes; those of *P. scilloides alba* are pure white. Both bloom in early spring. The strap-shaped leaves, ½ inch wide and up to 6 inches long, die back in summer. Striped squill combines well with crocuses, species tulips and snowdrops along woodland walks and under deciduous shrubs in containers on patios. Squills should be placed where their dainty flowers can be seen; heavy ground covers tend to overwhelm them.

HOW TO GROW. Striped squill is hardy in Zones 4-8, doing best in cool climates; where summers are hot it may need medium shade. It also needs protection from the wind. It grows well in sandy well-drained soil and requires little care. Plant bulbs in the fall, setting them 2 to 3 inches deep and 2 to 3 inches apart. They can be left undisturbed for years. In fact, moving may interrupt their blooming, so it is better to buy new bulbs than to divide existing plants.

Q

QUAKER LADIES See *Houstonia*

R

RABBIT'S FOOT FERN See *Polypodium*
REDBUD See *Cercis*

RHODODENDRON

R. calendulaceum (flame azalea); *R. carolinianum* (Carolina rhododendron); *R. kiusianum* (Kyushu azalea); *R. loderi* 'King George'; *R. schlippenbachii* (royal azalea); *R. 'Snowlady'; *R. williamsianum*

Rhododendrons and azaleas, which are among the most popular flowering plants for shade, are commonly thought to be, as a group, amenable to low-light conditions. In fact, all of them need some sun to produce the most profuse flowers, but some need more sun than others. The species and hybrids listed here bloom especially well in the minimal sun and bright light of open to medium shade, and two of them, Snowlady and the royal azalea, will even bloom in deep shade. Despite their physical differences, rhododendrons and azaleas belong to the same genus and require the same growing conditions. The four rhododendrons are all evergreen; two of the azaleas are deciduous and one is evergreen.

The flame azalea is a native American species, growing 4 to 6 feet high. It bears clusters of 2-inch clove-scented yellow to red-orange flowers in early summer, when most other azalea species have finished blooming. The leaves are 3 inches long and drop in the fall. Carolina rhododendron is a native American plant that grows wild in the Blue Ridge Mountains of North Carolina. It is 3 to 6 feet high with a naturally rounded shape and dark green leaves 3 inches long. In midspring it is covered with 3-inch clusters of rose-pink flowers. There is also a variety with pure white flowers and lighter green leaves, *R. carolinianum album*.

The Kyushu azalea is a low-growing Japanese species, only 18 inches high. Its leaves are deciduous when the plant is young but evergreen in maturity, remaining on the plant all winter, though often changing color. In its original form the Kyushu azalea is covered in midspring with 8- to 10-inch clusters of lilac pink flowers, but there are many named hybrids derived from this species. Benisuzume, for example, has red-orange flowers and red winter foliage; Hanekomachi has orchid-pink flowers with hairy bronze-green foliage.

King George is a tall hybrid rhododendron that blooms in midspring, producing huge pale pink flower clusters that turn white as they mature. It generally grows 6 feet tall but may reach a height of 12 feet. The royal azalea is a deciduous species, also of Japanese origin. It has soft green leaves that grow in whorls around the stem and turn yellow, orange and crimson in the fall. Its pink star-shaped flowers bloom in loose clusters in midspring and have a delicate fragrance.

Snowlady is a hybrid rhododendron that grows to a height of only 30 inches. It produces an abundance of snowy white flowers and has fuzzy green leaves. Somewhat taller than Snowlady is *R. williamsianum*, a species rhododendron that grows about 4 feet high. This dwarf plant forms attractive

FLAME AZALEA
Rhododendron calendulaceum

For climate zones and frost dates, see maps, pages 152-153.

CAROLINA RHODODENDRON
Rhododendron carolinianum

SALVIA
Salvia splendens 'Lavender Love'

mounds of bright green foliage and is haloed in midspring with pale pink bell-shaped flowers.

The larger rhododendrons and azaleas like King George and flame azalea make excellent specimen plants or informal groups in woodland settings, while smaller plants, such as the Carolina rhododendron, flourish in the shade of arbors and trellises. Snowlady, *R. williamsianum* and Kyushu azaleas can be used in the foreground of border plantings, and all three are also handsome pot plants for use in tubs or containers on shaded patios and terraces.

HOW TO GROW. Royal azalea is hardy in Zones 4-8; flame and Kyushu azaleas and Carolina rhododendron in Zones 5-8; and King George, Snowlady and *R. williamsianum* in Zones 7 and 8.

All rhododendrons thrive in a cool, moist, acid soil. Plant them in spring or fall where winter damage is no hazard; otherwise, plant them only in spring, setting the balled-and-burlaped root balls in the soil no deeper than 12 inches. Do not fertilize at the time of planting, as this might injure the roots, but water deeply. Supplemental feeding later is not normally needed, but if a plant appears pale or droopy, apply cottonseed meal or a fertilizer for acid-loving plants around its base in early spring. A year-round mulch of rotted oak leaves will also provide natural nutrients and will help keep the soil cool and moist.

Do not cultivate around the shallow roots of rhododendrons and azaleas, but pinch off their faded flowers to improve bloom the following year. Also, prune out dead, diseased or damaged branches, and cut old branches back to the soil level to encourage new growth.

Rhododendrons may be propagated from stem cuttings of new growth taken in late summer and rooted in a mixture of perlite or vermiculite and peat moss. For deciduous azaleas, cuttings may need bottom warmth of 75° and artificial light to promote root growth.

ROSE, CHRISTMAS See *Helleborus*
ROSE, LENTEN See *Helleborus*
ROYAL FERN See *Osmunda*

S

SAGE, SCARLET See *Salvia*

SALVIA
S. splendens (scarlet sage, salvia)

Traditionally a bedding plant for bright sun, scarlet sage has been bred in a number of white, purple and pink colors especially recommended for open shade. Some sunlight is needed for best growth, but too much sun will fade the flower colors. Although actually a tender perennial, scarlet sage is generally treated as an annual because it flowers from seed the first season, producing a continuous display of color from early summer until frost. The bushy, branching plants grow from 6 to 18 inches tall, with pointed oval leaves up to 3 inches long. The tubular flowers, ¾ to 1 inch long, grow in dense tiers around stems that rise above the foliage. Most varieties begin blooming six to eight weeks after sowing and are used to best advantage planted in masses.

Among the best varieties for shade are Lavender Love, which grows to 18 inches tall and bears long spikes of lavender flowers above lush, dark green foliage, and White Fire with creamy white flowers on an especially compact and bushy plant 14 inches tall. Purple Royal, also 14 inches tall, bears deep purple flowers, and a dwarf variety, Salmon Pygmy, grows only 6 inches tall and has early-blooming salmon-pink flowers.

HOW TO GROW. Although the pastel varieties of scarlet sage will grow in relatively poor soils, they do best in fertile well-drained garden soil with an even supply of moisture. Plant nursery-grown seedlings in the early spring, when all danger of frost is past, spacing them 8 to 12 inches apart. Seeds may be planted directly in the garden when night temperatures are consistently above 50°. Mulch in summer, if necessary, to maintain soil moisture.

SARCOCOCCA

S. hookeriana digyna (Himalayan sarcococca, sweet box, fragrant sarcococca); *S. hookeriana humilis* (dwarf Himalayan sarcococca)

Evergreen shrubs with year-round ornamental value, the Himalayan sarcococcas thrive in deep to open shade. The dense lance-shaped foliage is a bright, shiny green, 1½ to 4 inches long, and the tiny white flowers with conspicuous pollen-bearing stamens bloom from late winter until early spring. When the flowers fade, black berries ¼ inch wide decorate the branches into the following fall. The variety *digyna* is 4 to 6 feet tall with cream-colored stamens; the variety *humilis* is only 1 to 1½ feet tall, with pink stamens. Sarcococca spreads slowly on underground stems and may be grouped under taller shrubs and trees; the low-growing dwarf variety is also useful as a ground cover.

HOW TO GROW. Himalayan sarcococca is hardy in Zones 6-10, and the dwarf variety to Zone 5, but they need a location with some protection from wind to prevent winter damage to foliage. Both do best in a fairly rich, well-drained soil supplemented with 1 part of leaf mold or peat moss for every 2 parts of soil to improve drainage. Set out plants in early spring, spacing them 9 to 12 inches apart, depending on their ultimate size. Keep moist with a permanent mulch of wood chips, ground bark or chunky peat moss, 3 to 4 inches deep. Normally Himalayan sarcococcas do not need to be fertilized or pruned. Start new plants from cuttings taken in early summer or by dividing the roots of established plants in spring or late summer.

SAXIFRAGA

S. cortusifolia fortunei; S. stolonifera, also called *S. sarmentosa* (strawberry geranium); *S. umbrosa,* also called *S. serratifolia* (London pride) (all called saxifrage)

The saxifrages are low-growing rock plants, adapted by nature to open or dappled shade and valued for both their flowers and foliage. These three species are tender perennials with moundlike rosettes of leaves, and all of them spread by runners or underground stems to form matlike growth. They are used in rock-garden situations, such as on retaining walls or in crevices among paving stones, but they may also be used in woodland gardens as ground covers.

S. cortusifolia fortunei has thick, velvety leaves, kidney-shaped and composed of up to nine lobes. The leaves are 2 inches long and 4 inches wide, with the upper side green and the lower side reddish bronze; they form clumps 4 inches high. The 12-inch flower stems bear loose clusters of tiny fringed white flowers, only ½ inch long, in late fall or early winter. Plants spread by threadlike runners which take root to form new plants, carpeting an area 12 inches wide.

The strawberry geranium, also grown as a house plant, has round toothed-edged leaves up to 4 inches across. The leaves are reddish on the undersides, gray-green and hairy with white veins on the upper surfaces and form clumps 4 inches tall. The slender, branched flower stems are 18 to 24 inches tall and bear delicate white flowers 1 inch across. The variety Tricolor has leaves variegated with white and bright

HIMALAYAN SARCOCOCCA
Sarcococca hookeriana digyna

For climate zones and frost dates, see maps, pages 152-153.

141

STRAWBERRY GERANIUM
Saxifraga stolonifera

JAPANESE SKIMMIA
Skimmia japonica

pink. Plants spread by red, threadlike runners which take root to form new plants, carpeting an area 2 feet across.

London pride has stiff, leathery leaves that form clumps up to 6 inches tall. The elongated oval leaves, up to 2½ inches long, are gray-green on the surfaces and sometimes red on the undersides. From late spring until early summer, the 6-inch flower stems produce dainty sprays of white or pale pink flowers, each about ¼ inch across. There are many varieties of London pride, including Covillei with variegated pink and white flowers and Primuloides, with rose-colored flowers. London pride spreads on underground stems and is especially good for planting among paving stones.

HOW TO GROW. *S. cortusifolia fortunei,* strawberry geranium and London pride are hardy in Zones 7-9. Saxifrages grow best in garden soil liberally enriched with organic matter such as leaf mold, peat moss or compost. Excellent drainage is essential, but soil should remain evenly moist. A neutral soil should be maintained. Plant saxifrages in the spring, spacing them 8 to 10 inches apart. Mulch them lightly in winter to keep them from heaving out of the ground in areas with alternate freezing and thawing. Feed them in spring with an all-purpose garden fertilizer. Saxifrages may be propagated by collecting and sowing their seeds, but it is generally easier to start new plants by dividing plants after flowering or by moving rooted runners.

SENSITIVE FERN See *Onoclea*
SERVICEBERRY, APPLE See *Amelanchier*
SERVICEBERRY, DOWNY See *Amelanchier*
SHAD-BLOW See *Amelanchier*
SHADBUSH See *Amelanchier*
SIBERIAN TEA LEAVES See *Bergenia*
SILVER EDGE BISHOP'S WEED See *Aegopodium*
SILVER EDGE GOUTWEED See *Aegopodium*
SILVERY GLADE FERN See *Athyrium*

SKIMMIA
S. japonica (Japanese skimmia)

The ornamental, low-growing Japanese skimmia needs to be protected from the sun and is an ideal evergreen for decorating areas of open shade. It grows slowly into a rounded shrub, in three to four years reaching a height of 2 to 4 feet and a width of 3 to 6 feet. Its broad, shiny, leathery leaves are 3 to 4 inches long; in spring this foliage provides a background for 2- to 3-inch clusters of tiny yellow-white flowers. They are followed in the autumn by clusters of bright red berries. This species of skimmia requires that male and female plants be located within 100 feet of each other to produce berries. The berries appear only on the female plant, but the male plant has larger flowers, and its flowers are fragrant. Japanese skimmia berries often linger on the bush until flowers appear the following spring.

Skimmias are excellent foundation plants for the north side of buildings, and they are often combined with mountain laurels, whose culture is similar. Tolerant of city conditions such as smoke and dust and adaptable to containers, Japanese skimmia can brighten a shady urban terrace as a pot or tub plant, especially in one of its many dwarf forms.

HOW TO GROW. Japanese skimmia is hardy in Zones 7 and 8, although it may be planted in Zone 9 on the West Coast and north of Zone 7 along the East Coast when set in a protected spot. It needs a moist, well-drained acid soil, with 1 part peat moss or leaf mold added to every 2 parts of soil to improve drainage. When grown in pots, skimmias need a mixture of equal parts of sand, peat and loam. Plant them in early spring, 1½ to 3 feet apart. No fertilizing or pruning is usually necessary. To propagate skimmias, take 3- to 4-inch stem cuttings of male and female plants in spring or summer, and root them in sandy soil. Skimmias can be grown from seed, but it will not be possible to differentiate the males from the females until they flower. Seeds should be sown in sandy soil and kept at 70° until they germinate.

SNAKE'S HEAD See *Fritillaria*
SNOWFLAKE See *Leucojum*
SOURWOOD See *Oxydendrum*
SORREL TREE See *Oxydendrum*
SPIREA, FALSE See *Astilbe*
SPLEENWORT See *Asplenium*
SQUILL, STRIPED See *Puschkinia*
STRAWBERRY GERANIUM See *Saxifraga*
STRAWBERRY SHRUB See *Calycanthus*
SUMMER SWEET, PINK See *Clethra*
SWEET PEPPER BUSH See *Clethra*
SWEET SHRUB See *Calycanthus*

T

TAXUS

T. baccata 'Repandens' (spreading English yew, English weeping yew); *T. baccata* 'Stricta' (Irish yew); *T. canadensis* (Canada yew, ground-hemlock, American yew, ground yew); *T. cuspidata* 'Capitata' (upright Japanese yew); *T. media* 'Hicksii' (intermediate Hicks yew)

The hardy narrow-leaved evergreen yews are ideal landscape trees for almost any shade condition, from deep to open. All have dark green needles, and the female plants produce shiny red berries if a male yew is growing within 100 feet to allow pollination. The English yews are notable for their graceful shapes and rich coloring, the Irish yews for their compactness and slow growth, the Canada yews for their tolerance of shade, the Japanese yews for their sturdiness and weather resistance, the intermediate yews for their grace, color and hardiness. Although the yews are exceptionally attractive, the leaves, fruit and bark are poisonous.

The spreading English yew is a low, flat-topped shrub, growing slowly to 5 feet tall; its branches bend down at the tips. It is often used in the foreground of foundation plantings and does best in open shade. The Irish yew, an upright, columnar tree when young, becomes wider in maturity; it reaches a height of about 20 feet and has dense, dark green foliage. Irish yew makes a fine screen or specimen planting in medium to open shade. The Canada yew, a sprawling bush, rarely grows more than 3 feet tall. Its foliage is lighter than most other yews, and it is the best yew for heavily shaded areas; in fact, it is likely to turn brown in winter if grown in bright sun. It does not, however, have abundant berries. Canada yew is an excellent ground cover for use under thickly foliaged trees or in acid soil.

Upright Japanese yew is not as hardy as Canada yew but is hardier than English yew. Available in both fruiting and nonfruiting plants, it is a relatively fast-growing type whose shape is broadly conical. If unpruned, it may become 20 feet or more tall after 20 years in the garden in open shade. A profusely fruited tree, the intermediate Hicks yew resembles the Irish yew in habit of growth. Pillar-shaped, with many upraised branches, it eventually reaches a height of 18 feet after 25 years. It has very dark green foliage and is useful as a hedge or as a striking accent tree, alone or in combination with other plantings. It does best in open shade.

HOW TO GROW. Spreading English yew and Irish yew are hardy in Zones 6-8, Canada yew in Zones 3-8, upright Japanese yew in Zones 5-8 and intermediate Hicks yew in Zones

UPRIGHT JAPANESE YEW
Taxus cuspidata 'Capitata'

For climate zones and frost dates, see maps, pages 152-153.

WISHBONE FLOWER
Torenia fournieri

HAIRY TOAD LILY
Tricyrtis hirta

6-9. Yews grow best in rich, well-drained acid soil. Do not place them in continuously damp, soggy areas, however, such as near a downspout. Container-grown yews may be planted at any time, but freshly dug balled-and-burlaped yews should be planted in early spring. Set new plants in a mixture of 2 parts soil to 1 part peat moss and soak thoroughly. Allow generous space between plants for future growth. Fertilize newly planted trees with cottonseed meal or 5-10-5 fertilizer. Then fertilize again yearly in early spring. Yews can be pruned frequently when young to give them a more compact shape, but when they attain a desired height, prune them only once or twice a year. Severe pruning should only be done in early spring, before new growth starts.

TOAD LILY See *Tricyrtis*
TOBACCO, FLOWERING See *Nicotiana*

TORENIA

T. fournieri (blue wings, wishbone flower, torenia)

The violet- to blue-flowered torenias, as graceful in pots as they are in garden beds, are used to edge walks and patios in medium shade. These annuals, native to the tropics and semitropics, actually need to be protected from strong sunlight. They are bushy plants, about 1 foot tall, with oval tooth-edged leaves, 2 inches long, among which nestle tubular flowers, three or four to each wiry stalk. Each flower opens into two flaring lips, one pale violet, the other purplish blue, about 1 inch across. In the yellow-blotched throat are two pollen-bearing stamens shaped like a wishbone.

Viewed from above, the bicolored flowers, with their yellow throats, resemble pansies, and they are often planted with pansies because they begin to bloom in late spring, just as the pansies fade, and continue until the first frosts. A dwarf variety, *T. fournieri nana compacta,* grows densely to a height of only 8 inches and bears blue or white flowers.

HOW TO GROW. Torenias must be started indoors in Zones 3 and 4 to ensure a good crop of flowers before autumn frost. In Zones 5-10, they may be started either indoors or out. Indoors, sow seeds 10 to 12 weeks before the last spring frost is due, and keep the seedlings at about 65°; move them outdoors when night temperatures will remain above 60°. Sow seeds outdoors when all danger of frost has passed.

Set torenias 6 to 8 inches apart in any good garden soil and keep the ground moist. Support seedlings with bushy twigs stuck into the ground between them, and promote branching by pinching back the tips of the young plants.

TRICYRTIS

T. flava (yellow toad lily); *T. hirta* (hairy toad lily); *T. macropoda* (speckled toad lily)

Tender perennials for open shade, the toad lilies bloom in summer or fall, their intricately speckled flowers resting atop broad, flaring leaves like toads on lily pads. The flowers are trumpet-shaped, up to 1 inch long, and may be white, yellow or lavender with purple markings; the foliage is often hairy. Plants spread by means of rhizomes and are best suited to rock gardens or massed in perennial borders, where the late-blooming species add color when most flowers have faded.

Yellow toad lily, a small species, reaches a height of 12 to 20 inches and has 6-inch-long leaves that are sometimes spotted on the upper surface. The yellow flowers are dotted with dark purple or brown and bloom in late summer. Hairy toad lily has white or cream flowers spotted on the inside with purple; they are delicate, with a waxy texture. The leaves are 6 inches long. One variety, Variegata, has mottled foliage; another, Nigra, has dark spotted stems, and its flowers appear somewhat earlier in the fall. Speckled toad lily has white to lavender flowers speckled with dark purple spots; they are borne in clusters at the tips of the stems in midsummer. The plant grows 30 to 36 inches tall and has leaves that are 5 inches long.

HOW TO GROW. Yellow toad lily is hardy in Zones 7-10; hairy toad lily and speckled toad lily are hardy as far north as Zone 6, but should be planted in a sheltered location to minimize the danger of early frost. Toad lilies do best in moist garden loam enriched with organic matter such as peat moss, leaf mold or compost. Plant them in the spring or fall, spacing their rhizomes 12 to 18 inches apart. Feed them in spring with an all-purpose garden fertilizer. Prune off dead foliage in the late fall or early winter, and mulch after the first killing frost, using straw, salt hay or dry leaves. At the limits of their hardiness range, the roots may be dug up in the fall, dried, and stored over the winter like tender bulbs. Propagate by dividing the rhizomes in spring or fall.

TRILLIUM

T. erectum (purple trillium); *T. grandiflorum* (snow trillium, great white trillium)

Open shade suits the snow trillium, while purple trillium needs medium to deep shade. Both species are prized for their handsome flowers, which bloom in the spring and last up to a month. The plant's habit of growth also makes it useful as a ground cover in the shade garden—it spreads on creeping underground stems, or rhizomes, sending up dense clumps of foliage. The name trillium refers to the plant's structure, which is made up of threes: three petals, three sepals, three leaves. The latter are pointed ovals with indented veins, riding high on the stem, just below the single flower. In the fall, each flower produces a berry-like fruit.

Snow trillium bears 3- to 5-inch-wide flowers on stems 8 to 16 inches tall. The flowers are white or white tinged with pink, the white ones fading to pink, then to rose. Some varieties have double flowers. The leaves are 2½ to 6 inches long and a clear deep green; the fruit is blue-black. Each rhizome may send up as many as eight flower-bearing stems.

Purple trillium bears 1- to 3-inch-wide flowers on stems 6 to 24 inches tall. The flowers, which are actually maroon, have an unpleasant scent, but this is only noticeable at close range. The fruit is red; leaves are 5 to 7 inches long.

HOW TO GROW. Trilliums are hardy in Zones 3-8 and thrive in a moist, humus-rich soil. Snow trilliums grow best in a nearly neutral soil; purple trilliums prefer an acid soil. Plant trilliums in the fall, setting the rhizomes 2 to 4 inches deep with the eyes facing upward and spacing the plants 5 to 8 inches apart. Protect plants from cold and enrich the soil by adding a mulch of leaf mold or compost each winter. Propagate from seeds separated from the pulp and sown as soon as they ripen in the fall; they may take two years to germinate and another two years to bloom. Purple trilliums may also be propagated from offsets removed from the rhizomes when the plants are four to six years old.

TROUT LILY See *Erythronium*

TSUGA

T. canadensis (Canada hemlock); *T. canadensis pendula* (Sargent's weeping hemlock); *T. caroliniana* (Carolina hemlock)

Hemlocks are one of the few evergreens that will tolerate deep shade and they are also, by happy coincidence, among the most graceful of the conifers. The Canada hemlock is the hardiest species, often living for 200 to 500 years, but it does not do well under city conditions where the Carolina hem-

SNOW TRILLIUM
Trillium grandiflorum

For climate zones and frost dates, see maps, pages 152-153.

lock has greater tolerance. All three species listed here can be planted in the shade of tall deciduous trees, and they also are useful for plantings on the north side of buildings. Since they are easily pruned, hemlocks make excellent hedges or screens in shaded areas. The Carolina hemlock is, in addition, a good freestanding ornamental specimen but should not be exposed to winter winds. Sargent's weeping hemlock may be used in tubs on shaded terraces or under arbors.

The Canada hemlock is a fast-growing upright tree with an irregularly rounded shape; it has drooping branches and eventually becomes 65 feet or more tall. Its needles are short, only ⅜ inch long, and it has small oval 1-inch cones that are long lasting. Sargent's weeping hemlock grows to 15 feet tall and after 25 to 50 years becomes nearly three times as broad as it is high. Flat topped when young, with cascading branches, it becomes dome shaped when mature. Carolina hemlock reaches a height of 15 to 40 feet tall in 15 to 20 years. Its soft, dark green ¾-inch needles grow in thick whorls around its stems; it bears 1½-inch cones. Canada and Sargent's weeping hemlock are hardy in Zones 3-8, Carolina hemlock in Zones 5-8.

HOW TO GROW. Hemlocks do best where the soil is cool, moist and acid, and where the air is damp, with abundant rainfall. They do not grow well where summers are long, hot and dry. Because they are shallow rooted, hemlocks are easily transplanted if a ball of soil is left around the roots. Fertilize them only if the foliage is sparse and pale, dusting cottonseed meal around the base in early spring. They may be pruned at any time, but their foliage is most flexible and new shoots grow most readily in spring and early summer.

V

VIBURNUM

V. acerifolium (maple-leaved viburnum, dockmackie); *V. dentatum* (arrowwood, southern arrowwood); *V. plicatum tomentosum mariesii* (Maries' doublefile viburnum) (Japanese snowball); *V. prunifolium* (black haw) (all called viburnum)

Viburnums are among the few flowering shrubs that bloom even in deep shade. Most of them produce abundant flowers in open to medium shade, but for the most lavish display of blossoms they need some sun in spring. These four species are especially noted for their tolerance of shade; they range from 4 feet to about 15 feet tall. All have dark green coarsely toothed leaves that change color before they drop in fall. Viburnums bear two kinds of white flowers: fertile blossoms that bloom in flat clusters and produce edible berries and sterile ones with ball-shaped clusters that produce no fruit. All four of these species are flat clustered and fruiting.

Maple-leaved viburnum grows 3 to 5 feet tall, spreading 3 or 4 feet wide. Its maple-like three-lobed leaves, 2 to 4 inches long, turn red in fall. Its clusters of fertile white flowers, 2 to 3 inches wide, appear in early summer, followed in the fall by ¼-inch purple-black fruit. In deep shade it blooms lightly and is most valued for its autumn color. Arrowwood is a bushy shrub 10 to 15 feet tall and 6 to 8 feet wide. Its 1½- to 3-inch-long leaves turn rusty red in fall. Its 2- to 3-inch flower clusters open in late spring or early summer; the ¼-inch blue-black berries ripen in fall. This species spreads rapidly and is a useful filler for borders in open shade, especially when planted in groups.

Japanese snowball grows 5 to 7 feet tall, bearing 2- to 3-inch ball-shaped clusters of sterile white flowers in late spring. A variety, Maries' doublefile viburnum, also has berries that turn from red to black as they ripen in midsummer. The 2- to 4-inch leaves turn purplish-red in the fall. Black haw grows 10 to 15 feet tall, with a spread about three

CANADA HEMLOCK
Tsuga canadensis

quarters as wide. Its dark green leaves, 2 to 3 inches long, turn purple-red in the fall. Its flat 2- to 4-inch flower clusters appear in midspring, followed in early fall by ½-inch blue-black berries. Black haw, a popular accent for open to medium shade, is often used instead of hawthorn, which it resembles without having hawthorn's susceptibility to pests.

HOW TO GROW. Arrowwood is hardy in Zones 3-8; Japanese snowball, black haw and maple-leaved viburnum grow in Zones 4-8. All of them do well in almost any well-drained soil but are most at home in a cool, moist soil. They can be purchased and planted at any time in any form: bare rooted, container grown or balled and burlaped. For informal hedges of lower-growing species, space plants 2½ to 4 feet apart. Viburnums normally do not need fertilizing. Limit pruning to the removal of dead branches. Prune Japanese snowball and black haw in late spring or early summer immediately after flowering; prune arrowwood and maple-leaved viburnum in late winter or early spring. Propagate from cuttings of new growth in late spring or early summer.

VINCA
V. minor (common periwinkle, creeping myrtle)

Common periwinkle is a hardy evergreen ground cover that thrives in any kind of shade, dappled to dense, open to covered. Its flowers are somewhat fewer, however, when it is grown in low light. The plant's crisscrossing stems, 1 to 2 feet long, interlock to form a low mat, up to 6 inches tall, of shiny pointed leaves ½ to ¾ inch long. Lavender-blue flowers 1 inch across begin to bloom at the stem tips in early spring, often continuing to flower at intervals until fall. The variety Bowles has large blue flowers and dark green foliage; Alba has white flowers; Atropurpurea, dark purple flowers; and Punicea or Burgundy, red-purple flowers. In addition, some varieties have mottled leaves: Argenteo Variegata has white-edged leaves and Aurea Variegata has yellow-edged leaves. All types of common periwinkle spread rapidly by rooting wherever their stems touch moist ground. They are suitable for planting at the bases of trees, along paths or as covering for sloping banks.

HOW TO GROW. Common periwinkle is hardy in Zones 5-10. It tolerates any soil but does best in deep, rich, moist soil enriched with 1 part leaf mold or peat moss for every 2 parts of soil. Set out plants 12 to 18 inches apart in spring or early fall. Keep the ground moist, and fertilize with a light sprinkling of all-purpose fertilizer in early spring until plants are established. Propagate by dividing old plants in spring or from rooted stem cuttings at any time.

VIOLA
V. labradorica (Labrador violet); *V. odorata* (sweet violet, florists' violet); *V. striata* (pale violet)

Most members of the violet family—some 500 species strong—are spring-blooming woodland perennials that grow in open shade. They make good ground covers, filling in the bare spots beneath shrubs, and they may also be used as edging plants for borders or in rock gardens. Their flowers are similar to those of pansies in shape, but they are generally a single color, smaller and longer lasting. Violets spread fairly rapidly by seeding themselves, by creeping roots and by surface runners, which can be a problem in a lawn.

From among many desirable species, the tiny Labrador violet and the large pale violet represent the available size range, and the sweet violet is the most fragrant. Labrador violets grow up to 3 inches high with a few short stems bearing round, smooth leaves, ¾ inch across, and deep violet flowers. Sweet violets grow 8 inches tall, their 1½-inch oval

MARIES' DOUBLEFILE VIBURNUM
Viburnum plicatum tomentosum mariesii

COMMON PERIWINKLE
Vinca minor

For climate zones and frost dates, see maps, pages 152-153.

147

SWEET VIOLET
Viola odorata

CRIMSON GLORY VINE
Vitis coignetiae

leaves rising in clumps from long runners. The ¾-inch flowers, source of oils used by the perfume industry, are intensely fragrant and have been hybridized in many shades of purple, blue, rose and white. Some of these hybrids are double flowered, and many have a second period of bloom in the fall. Pale violets grow in tufts or clusters, with stems up to 2 feet long. Their 2-inch leaves are oval to round, with toothed edges, and the ¾-inch flowers are white or cream with delicate blue or purple veins; sometimes the centers of the flowers are tinted rose.

HOW TO GROW. Labrador and pale violets are hardy in Zones 4-8; sweet violets in Zones 7-10. They grow best in well-drained humus-rich soil that is slightly acid. Pale violet and sweet violet require a moist soil; Labrador violet tolerates drier conditions. Set out plants in the spring or fall, spacing the clumps 6 to 12 inches apart with the tops of the roots at ground level. Mulch them with leaf mold, but apply only a thin layer to tiny Labrador violets to avoid smothering them. Violets may be easily propagated from seed sown in the fall or by root division in early spring or fall.

VIOLET See *Viola*
VIRGINIA CREEPER See *Parthenocissus*
VIRGIN'S BOWER See *Clematis*

VITIS
V. coignetiae (crimson glory vine)

The perennial crimson glory vine adapts itself to open shade, twining its tendrils rapidly around a vertical support and growing as much as 30 feet a year to a maximum height of 60 to 90 feet. Its bold heart-shaped leaves, up to a foot long and nearly as wide, provide a dense cover for walls, arbors, trellises or fences. The vine's foliage is thick, coarsely toothed and divided into three or five lobes. Smooth and green above, downy and rust-red on the undersides, it turns bright scarlet and crimson in autumn. Inconspicuous purple flowers bloom in late spring, followed by clusters of ½-inch black grapelike fruit, which is inedible.

HOW TO GROW. Crimson glory vine is hardy in Zones 6-9 and grows in any moist, well-drained garden soil. Plant young vines in late fall or early spring, while they are dormant, adding compost to the soil at planting time. Support young plants with canes or stakes and train them up vertical supports, such as wires spaced 1 to 2 feet apart or trellises. Pinch back growing tips to encourage branching. Keep soil moist and spread a layer of compost around the base of the plant each spring. Prune and thin in late summer to control growth. Propagate from seeds sown in a cold frame or outdoors in early winter or by fastening a stem to the ground during the growing season until it takes root.

W

WALL FERN See *Polypodium*
WAND PLANT See *Galax*
WANDFLOWER See *Galax*
WILD GINGER See *Asarum*
WINTER ACONITE See *Eranthis*
WINTER CREEPER See *Euonymus*
WINTER HAZEL See *Corylopsis*
WINTERGREEN See *Gaultheria*
WISH BONE FLOWER See *Torenia*
WITCH ALDER See *Fothergilla*
WOODBINE See *Parthenocissus*

Y

YEW See *Taxus*

Appendix

Characteristics of 108 shade-garden plants

Listed below for quick reference are the species illustrated in Chapter 5.

	PLANT HEIGHT				TYPE OF SHADE			SPECIAL TRAITS				FLOWER COLOR				FLOWER SEASON				SOIL NEEDS				
	Under 1 foot	1 to 3 feet	3 to 6 feet	Over 6 feet	Deep shade	Medium shade	Open or intermittent shade	Distinctive foliage	Evergreen	Flowers	Fruit	White to green	Yellow to orange	Pink to red	Blue to purple	Spring	Summer	Fall	Winter	Acid	Alkaline	Dry	Moist but well drained	Wet
ANNUALS																								
BEGONIA GRANDIS (hardy begonia)		●				●				●				●		●	●						●	
BEGONIA SEMPERFLORENS (wax begonia)	●					●				●		●		●		●	●	●	●				●	
BEGONIA TUBERHYBRIDA 'DOUBLE RUFFLED APRICOT' (tuberous begonia)		●				●				●			●				●						●	
BROWALLIA SPECIOSA MAJOR 'BLUE TROLL' (blue troll browallia)	●					●				●					●		●						●	
COLEUS HYBRID 'ROSE WIZARD' (rose wizard coleus)	●					●	●	●						●			●						●	
DIGITALIS PURPUREA (foxglove)		●				●				●		●	●	●	●		●						●	
IMPATIENS BALSAMINA (garden balsam)	●	●			●	●				●		●		●	●	●	●	●					●	
IMPATIENS WALLERANA (patient Lucy)	●	●			●	●				●		●	●	●	●	●	●						●	
LOBULARIA MARITIMA (sweet alyssum)	●					●				●		●			●		●	●		●			●	
MIMULUS CUPREUS (monkey flower)	●	●				●				●		●	●	●			●	●					●	
MIMULUS HYBRIDUS (monkey flower)	●	●				●				●		●	●	●			●	●					●	
MYOSOTIS SYLVATICA (woodland forget-me-not)	●	●			●	●				●					●	●	●						●	
NEMOPHILA MENZIESII (baby-blue-eyes)	●					●				●					●	●	●						●	
NICOTIANA ALATA 'NICKI RED' (flowering tobacco)		●				●				●				●			●						●	
SALVIA SPLENDENS 'LAVENDER LOVE' (salvia)		●				●				●				●			●	●					●	
TORENIA FOURNIERI (wishbone flower)		●			●					●				●	●	●	●	●					●	
BROAD-LEAVED EVERGREEN SHRUBS																								
ABELIA GRANDIFLORA (glossy abelia)			●			●		●	●	●		●				●	●		●				●	
CAMELLIA JAPONICA (common camellia)				●		●			●	●				●		●			●	●			●	
ILEX AQUIFOLIUM (English holly)			●	●			●		●		●								●	●			●	
KALMIA LATIFOLIA (mountain laurel)			●	●		●			●	●		●		●		●				●			●	
LEUCOTHOË FONTANESIANA (drooping leucothoë)		●		●	●	●			●	●		●				●				●			●	
PAXISTIMA CANBYI (Canby pachistima)	●					●	●	●					●			●				●			●	
PIERIS JAPONICA (Japanese andromeda)		●				●	●	●	●				●			●				●			●	
RHODODENDRON CAROLINIANUM (Carolina rhododendron)		●				●	●		●	●				●		●				●			●	
SARCOCOCCA HOOKERIANA DIGYNA (Himalayan sarcococca)		●			●	●	●	●	●	●	●					●			●	●			●	
SKIMMIA JAPONICA (Japanese skimmia)		●	●			●	●	●	●	●	●					●			●	●			●	
BULBS																								
CALADIUM HORTULANUM 'CANDIDUM' (candidum fancy-leaved caladium)		●				●	●	●		●				●			●						●	
CONVALLARIA MAJALIS (lily of the valley)	●				●	●	●			●		●				●				●			●	
ERANTHIS HYEMALIS (winter aconite)	●				●	●		●		●			●			●			●				●	
ERYTHRONIUM 'PAGODA' (Pagoda fawn lily)	●				●	●		●		●			●			●							●	
FRITILLARIA MELEAGRIS (checkered fritillary)	●					●		●		●			●			●	●						●	
LEUCOJUM VERNUM (spring snowflake)		●				●		●		●		●				●							●	
LILIUM MARTAGON (martagon lily)			●			●		●		●			●				●						●	
LILIUM TESTACEUM (Nankeen lily)				●		●		●		●			●				●						●	
MUSCARI TUBERGENIANUM (grape hyacinth)	●					●		●		●					●	●							●	
PUSCHKINIA SCILLOIDES (striped squill)	●				●	●		●		●		●			●	●							●	
DECIDUOUS SHRUBS																								
ARONIA ARBUTIFOLIA BRILLIANTISSIMA (brilliant chokeberry)			●	●			●			●	●	●				●				●			●	
CALYCANTHUS FLORIDUS (sweet shrub)			●			●	●	●	●		●			●			●						●	

149

	PLANT HEIGHT				TYPE OF SHADE			SPECIAL TRAITS				FLOWER COLOR				FLOWER SEASON				SOIL NEEDS				
	Under 1 foot	1 to 3 feet	3 to 6 feet	Over 6 feet	Deep shade	Medium shade	Open or intermittent shade	Distinctive foliage	Evergreen	Flowers	Fruit	White to green	Yellow to orange	Pink to red	Blue to purple	Spring	Summer	Fall	Winter	Acid	Alkaline	Dry	Moist but well drained	Wet
CLETHRA ALNIFOLIA 'ROSEA' (pink summer sweet)		●				●	●			●			●			●				●			●	
CORYLOPSIS SPICATA (spike winter hazel)		●			●	●				●			●			●				●			●	
ENKIANTHUS CAMPANULATUS (redvein enkianthus)			●		●	●				●		●	●			●				●			●	
FOTHERGILLA MAJOR (large fothergilla)			●		●	●				●		●				●				●			●	
HYDRANGEA MACROPHYLLA 'SILVER VARIEGATED MARIESII' (big-leaved hydrangea)		●			●	●	●			●					●	●				●			●	
KERRIA JAPONICA 'PLENIFLORA' (globeflower kerria)		●	●	●	●	●				●			●			●	●	●					●	
RHODODENDRON CALENDULACEUM (flame azalea)		●			●	●				●			●	●		●				●			●	
VIBURNUM PLICATUM TOMENTOSUM MARIESII (Maries' doublefile viburnum)		●	●	●	●	●	●			●	●	●				●							●	

FERNS

	Under 1 foot	1 to 3 feet	3 to 6 feet	Over 6 feet	Deep shade	Medium shade	Open or intermittent shade	Distinctive foliage	Evergreen	Flowers	Fruit	White to green	Yellow to orange	Pink to red	Blue to purple	Spring	Summer	Fall	Winter	Acid	Alkaline	Dry	Moist but well drained	Wet
ADIANTUM PEDATUM (northern maidenhair)	●	●			●	●	●	●												●			●	
ASPLENIUM BULBIFERUM (mother fern)		●			●			●												●			●	
ASPLENIUM TRICHOMANES (maidenhair spleenwort)	●				●	●	●	●												●		●		
ATHYRIUM GOERINGIANUM PICTUM (Japanese painted fern)		●			●	●	●	●												●			●	
DENNSTAEDTIA PUNCTILOBULA (hay-scented fern)		●			●	●	●	●														●	●	●
ONOCLEA SENSIBILIS (sensitive fern)		●	●			●	●	●												●				●
OSMUNDA REGALIS (royal fern)			●		●	●	●	●												●				●
POLYPODIUM SCOULERI (leathery polypody)		●				●		●												●		●		
POLYPODIUM VULGARE (common polypody)	●						●	●												●		●		

GROUND COVERS

	Under 1 foot	1 to 3 feet	3 to 6 feet	Over 6 feet	Deep shade	Medium shade	Open or intermittent shade	Distinctive foliage	Evergreen	Flowers	Fruit	White to green	Yellow to orange	Pink to red	Blue to purple	Spring	Summer	Fall	Winter	Acid	Alkaline	Dry	Moist but well drained	Wet
AEGOPODIUM PODAGRARIA 'VARIEGATUM' (silveredge goutweed)	●	●			●	●	●	●		●		●					●			●	●	●	●	●
AJUGA REPTANS (bugleweed)	●				●	●	●	●		●				●	●					●	●	●	●	●
BERGENIA CRASSIFOLIA (leather bergenia)	●					●	●	●						●	●		●			●			●	
CORNUS CANADENSIS (bunchberry)	●					●		●		●	●	●				●				●				●
DICHONDRA REPENS (dichondra)	●					●	●																●	
EPIMEDIUM GRANDIFLORUM (bishop's hat)	●				●	●	●	●		●		●		●	●	●				●			●	
EUONYMUS FORTUNEI COLORATUS (purple winter creeper)	●					●	●	●	●											●			●	
FESTUCA OVINA GLAUCA (blue fescue)	●					●		●														●		
GALAX APHYLLA (galax)	●				●	●	●	●		●		●				●	●			●			●	
GAULTHERIA PROCUMBENS (wintergreen)	●					●	●	●	●	●	●	●		●			●			●			●	
LYSIMACHIA NUMMULARIA (moneywort)	●				●	●	●	●		●			●				●			●			●	
MAHONIA REPENS (creeping Mahonia)		●				●		●	●	●	●		●			●				●			●	
OPHIOPOGON JAPONICUS (dwarf lily-turf)	●					●	●	●	●	●	●				●					●			●	
PACHYSANDRA TERMINALIS (pachysandra)	●					●	●	●	●	●	●					●				●			●	
VINCA MINOR (common periwinkle)	●				●	●	●	●	●						●	●	●	●					●	

NEEDLED EVERGREEN SHRUBS

	Under 1 foot	1 to 3 feet	3 to 6 feet	Over 6 feet	Deep shade	Medium shade	Open or intermittent shade	Distinctive foliage	Evergreen	Flowers	Fruit	White to green	Yellow to orange	Pink to red	Blue to purple	Spring	Summer	Fall	Winter	Acid	Alkaline	Dry	Moist but well drained	Wet
TAXUS CUSPIDATA 'CAPITATA' (upright Japanese yew)			●	●	●	●	●	●	●		●									●		●		
TSUGA CANADENSIS (Canada hemlock)			●	●	●	●	●	●	●											●		●		

PERENNIALS

	Under 1 foot	1 to 3 feet	3 to 6 feet	Over 6 feet	Deep shade	Medium shade	Open or intermittent shade	Distinctive foliage	Evergreen	Flowers	Fruit	White to green	Yellow to orange	Pink to red	Blue to purple	Spring	Summer	Fall	Winter	Acid	Alkaline	Dry	Moist but well drained	Wet
ASTILBE ARENDSII 'ROSY VEIL' (astilbe)		●			●	●	●			●				●			●						●	
CORYDALIS LUTEA (yellow corydalis)		●			●	●	●			●			●			●	●					●		
DICENTRA CUCULLARIA (Dutchman's breeches)	●					●	●			●		●				●				●			●	
HELLEBORUS NIGER (Christmas rose)		●					●		●	●		●							●	●			●	

Plant	Under 1 foot	1 to 3 feet	3 to 6 feet	Over 6 feet	Deep shade	Medium shade	Open or intermittent shade	Distinctive foliage	Evergreen	Flowers	Fruit	White to green	Yellow to orange	Pink to red	Blue to purple	Spring	Summer	Fall	Winter	Acid	Alkaline	Dry	Moist but well drained	Wet
	PLANT HEIGHT				**TYPE OF SHADE**			**SPECIAL TRAITS**				**FLOWER COLOR**				**FLOWER SEASON**				**SOIL NEEDS**				
HEMEROCALLIS HYBRID (day lily)		•			•		•			•			•		•	•	•	•					•	
HOSTA UNDULATA 'MEDIO-PICTA' (hosta)		•				•		•		•				•			•						•	
IRIS CRISTATA (crested iris)	•						•			•				•	•					•			•	
PRIMULA SIEBOLDII (Siebold's primrose)	•						•			•				•		•				•			•	
SAXIFRAGA STOLONIFERA (strawberry geranium)	•						•	•		•	•			•		•	•						•	
TRICRYTIS HIRTA (hairy toad lily)		•					•			•	•							•					•	

TREES

Plant	Under 1 foot	1 to 3 feet	3 to 6 feet	Over 6 feet	Deep shade	Medium shade	Open or intermittent shade	Distinctive foliage	Evergreen	Flowers	Fruit	White to green	Yellow to orange	Pink to red	Blue to purple	Spring	Summer	Fall	Winter	Acid	Alkaline	Dry	Moist but well drained	Wet
ACER PALMATUM ATROPURPUREUM (blood-leaved Japanese maple)				•		•	•																•	
AMELANCHIER GRANDIFLORA (apple serviceberry)				•			•	•	•	•						•							•	
CERCIS CANADENSIS (eastern redbud)				•		•	•			•				•		•							•	
CORNUS NUTTALLII (mountain dogwood)				•		•	•	•	•	•						•				•			•	
CHIONANTHUS VIRGINICUS (fringe tree)				•		•	•			•						•							•	
OXYDENDRUM ARBOREUM (sorrel tree)				•			•			•								•		•			•	

VINES

Plant	Under 1 foot	1 to 3 feet	3 to 6 feet	Over 6 feet	Deep shade	Medium shade	Open or intermittent shade	Distinctive foliage	Evergreen	Flowers	Fruit	White to green	Yellow to orange	Pink to red	Blue to purple	Spring	Summer	Fall	Winter	Acid	Alkaline	Dry	Moist but well drained	Wet
ARISTOLOCHIA DURIOR (Dutchman's pipe)				•		•	•	•		•			•	•									•	
CLEMATIS JACKMANII (clematis)				•		•	•	•		•					•		•	•			•		•	
HEDERA HELIX (English ivy)				•		•		•	•														•	
JASMINUM OFFICINALE (common white jasmine)				•			•			•	•						•						•	
LONICERA JAPONICA 'HALLIANA' (Hall's Japanese honeysuckle)				•			•	•	•	•	•												•	
PARTHENOCISSUS QUINQUEFOLIA (woodbine)				•	•	•	•	•		•	•	•						•					•	
VITIS COIGNETIAE (crimson glory vine)				•		•	•	•		•	•				•	•							•	

WILDFLOWERS

Plant	Under 1 foot	1 to 3 feet	3 to 6 feet	Over 6 feet	Deep shade	Medium shade	Open or intermittent shade	Distinctive foliage	Evergreen	Flowers	Fruit	White to green	Yellow to orange	Pink to red	Blue to purple	Spring	Summer	Fall	Winter	Acid	Alkaline	Dry	Moist but well drained	Wet
AQUILEGIA CANADENSIS (American columbine)		•				•	•			•		•	•	•	•	•	•						•	
ARISAEMA TRIPHYLLUM (Jack-in-the-pulpit)		•			•	•	•	•		•	•	•				•				•			•	
ASARUM CANADENSE (Canada wild ginger)	•				•	•		•		•						•				•			•	
CIMICIFUGA SIMPLEX 'WHITE PEARL' (Kamchatka bugbane)		•	•		•	•	•			•		•							•	•			•	
CYPRIPEDIUM REGINAE (showy lady's slipper)		•			•	•	•			•		•					•			•			•	
GERANIUM MACULATUM (spotted geranium)		•					•			•				•		•	•			•			•	
HOUSTONIA CAERULEA (bluet)	•						•			•					•	•				•			•	
LOBELIA CARDINALIS (cardinal flower)		•	•				•			•				•			•	•		•			•	
MERTENSIA VIRGINICA (Virginia bluebell)		•			•	•				•				•	•	•				•			•	
PHLOX DIVARICATA (wild sweet William)	•	•					•			•				•	•	•				•			•	
PODOPHYLLUM PELTATUM (common May apple)		•					•			•	•					•				•			•	
TRILLIUM GRANDIFLORUM (snow trillium)	•	•					•			•	•	•				•				•			•	
VIOLA ODORATA (sweet violet)	•						•			•				•	•	•				•			•	

The where and when of shade plantings

Shade plants, like their sun-loving relatives, have definite temperature preferences; indeed, they are sometimes even more sensitive to heat and cold —partly because their foliage is in effect thin-skinned, without the tough protective covering that shields sun plants from solar heat. Because of this, the foregoing encyclopedia of shade plants specifies climate zones, keyed to the map below, wherever that information is important. It is well to remember, however, that shade temperatures may vary from the norm depending on such factors as elevation or exposure to prevailing winds. If it is cold on a sunny hillside, for instance, it may be even colder on a shaded one, but the temperature will be less subject to rapid fluctuations.

The normal dates of first and last frosts for a specific area, given on the maps at right, may also vary in shade gardens. Spring often comes later, especially under evergreen trees or on the north side of a wall. With no sun to warm it, the soil temperature may be 15 degrees lower than that of the open garden. But this delayed arrival has its blessings. Shade plants are less prone to the thawing and freezing that can break roots and even force plants from the soil. In addition, fallen leaves form a blanket that protects the roots of early-blooming plants such as spring bulbs and wildflowers. Trees such as star magnolia and flowering dogwood bloom later in the shade, when there is less danger of damage from a late frost.

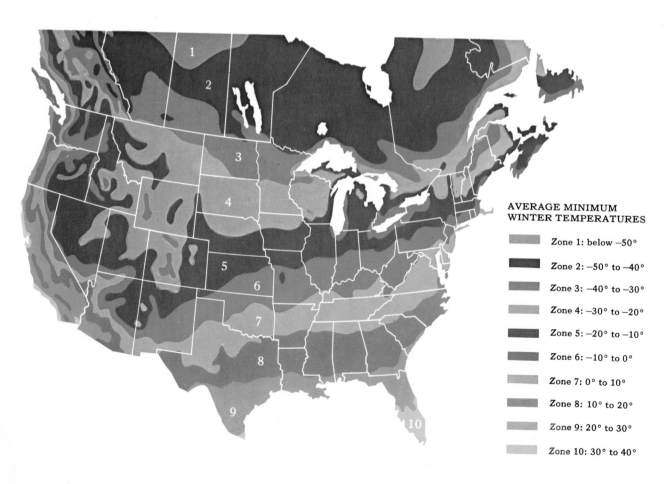

AVERAGE MINIMUM WINTER TEMPERATURES

Zone 1: below −50°

Zone 2: −50° to −40°

Zone 3: −40° to −30°

Zone 4: −30° to −20°

Zone 5: −20° to −10°

Zone 6: −10° to 0°

Zone 7: 0° to 10°

Zone 8: 10° to 20°

Zone 9: 20° to 30°

Zone 10: 30° to 40°

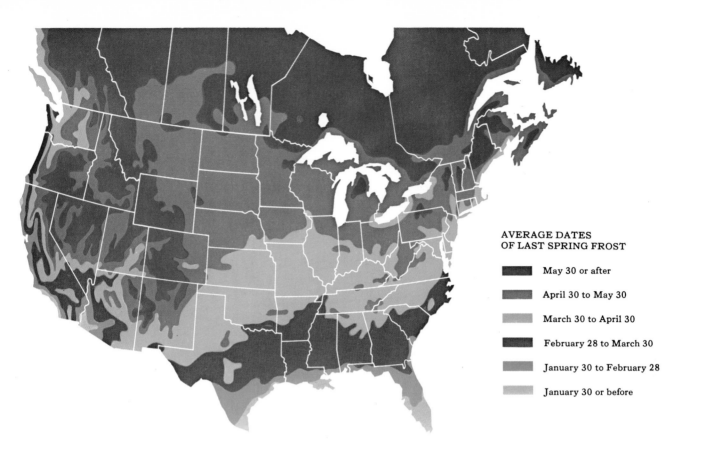

AVERAGE DATES
OF LAST SPRING FROST

May 30 or after

April 30 to May 30

March 30 to April 30

February 28 to March 30

January 30 to February 28

January 30 or before

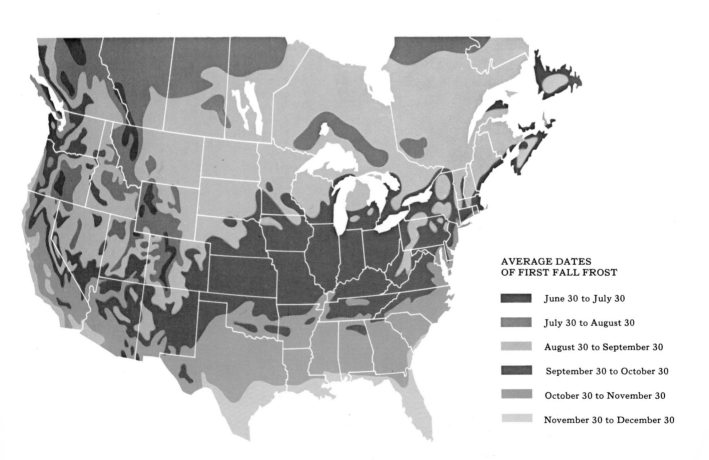

AVERAGE DATES
OF FIRST FALL FROST

June 30 to July 30

July 30 to August 30

August 30 to September 30

September 30 to October 30

October 30 to November 30

November 30 to December 30

Bibliography

Atkinson, Dr. Robert E., *The Complete Book of Ground-covers: Lawns You Don't Have to Mow.* David McKay Co., Inc., 1970.

Bailey, L. H., *Standard Cyclopedia of Horticulture.* The Macmillan Co., 1935.

Bartrum, Douglas, *Climbing Plants and Some Shrubs.* John Gifford Ltd., 1958.

Birdseye, Clarence and Eleanor G., *Growing Woodland Plants.* Dover Publications, Inc., 1972.

Bland, John H., *Forests of Lilliput.* Prentice-Hall, 1971.

Bonner, James, and Galston, Arthur W., *Principles of Plant Physiology.* W. H. Freeman and Co., 1952.

Brilmayer, Bernice, *All About Vines and Hanging Plants.* Doubleday & Co., Inc., 1962.

Brooklyn Botanic Garden, *Gardening in the Shade.* BBG, 1969.

Brooklyn Botanic Garden, *The Home Lawn Handbook.* BBG, 1973.

Brooklyn Botanic Garden, *Perennials and Their Uses.* BBG, 1978.

Brown, Ron, *Flowering Shrubs.* Ward Lock Ltd., 1970.

Busch, Phyllis S., *Wildflowers and the Stories Behind Their Names.* Charles Scribner's Sons, 1977.

Bush-Brown, James and Louise, *Garden Book.* Charles Scribner's Sons, 1958.

Chittenden, Fred J., ed., *The Royal Horticultural Society Dictionary of Gardening,* 2nd ed. Clarendon Press, 1974.

Coats, Alice M., *Flowers and Their Histories.* McGraw-Hill Book Co., 1971.

Cronquist, Arthur, *Introductory Botany.* Harper & Row, Publishers, 1961.

Cruso, Thalassa, *Making Things Grow Outdoors.* Alfred A. Knopf, 1976.

Dietz, Marjorie J., ed., *10,000 Garden Questions Answered by 20 Experts.* Doubleday & Co., Inc., 1974.

Duble, Richard, and Kell, James Carroll, *Southern Lawns and Groundcovers.* Pacesetter Press, 1977.

Everett, T. H., *Lawns & Lawnscaping.* Grosset & Dunlap, 1975.

Fish, Margery, *Gardening in the Shade.* W. H. & L. Collingridge Ltd., 1964.

Fisk, J., *Success With Clematis.* Thomas Nelson and Sons Ltd., 1962.

Fletcher, H. L. V., *Popular Flowering Shrubs.* Drake Publishers Inc., 1972.

Fogg, H. G. Witham, *History of Popular Garden Plants From A to Z.* A. S. Barnes & Co., Inc., 1977.

Foley, Daniel J., *Ground Covers for Easier Gardening.* Dover Publications, Inc., 1972.

Foster, F. Gordon, *Ferns to Know and Grow.* Hawthorn Books, 1971.

Givens, Harold, *Landscape It Yourself.* Harcourt Brace Jovanovich, 1977.

Gleason, Henry A., *The New Britton and Brown Illustrated Flora of the Northeastern United States and Adjacent Canada,* vol. 3. The New York Botanical Garden, 1952.

Haworth-Booth, Michael, *The Hydrangeas.* Constable and Co., Ltd., 1959.

Hebb, Robert S., *Low Maintenance Perennials.* Quadrangle, 1975.

Hoshizaki, Barbara Joe, *Fern Growers Manual.* Alfred A. Knopf, 1975.

Hottes, Alfred C., *A Little Book of Climbing Plants.* A. T. De La Mare Co., Inc., 1933.

Howard, Frances, *Landscaping With Vines.* The Macmillan Co., 1959.

Klaber, Doretta, *Primroses and Spring.* M. Barrows & Co., 1966.

McCollon, William C., *Vines and How to Grow Them.* Doubleday, 1911.

Menninger, Edwin A., *Flowering Vines of the World: An Encyclopedia of Climbing Plants.* Hearthside Press, Inc., 1970.

Montgomery, Guy, ed., *Bacon's Essays.* The Macmillan Co., 1930.

Morse, H. K., *Gardening in the Shade.* Charles Scribner's Sons, 1939.

Nelson, William R., Jr., *Landscaping Your Home.* University of Illinois Press, 1975.

Ohwi, Jisaburo, *Flora of Japan,* Frederick G. Meyer and Egbert H. Walker, eds. Smithsonian Institution, 1965.

Ortloff, H. Stuart, *The Book of Landscape Design.* William Morrow & Co., Inc., 1975.

Parcher, Emily S., *Shady Gardens.* Prentice-Hall, 1955.

Pierot, Suzanne, *The Ivy Book.* Macmillan Publishing Co., Inc., 1974.

Pierot, Suzanne Warner, *What Can I Grow in the Shade?* Liveright, 1977.

Preston, Richard J., Jr., *North American Trees.* The Iowa State University Press, 1969.

Reader's Digest Association, ed., *Reader's Digest Encyclopedia of Garden Plants and Flowers.* Reader's Digest Association, Ltd., 1975.

Rockwell, F. F., and Grayson, Esther C., *The Complete Book of Bulbs.* Lippincott, 1977.

Schuler, Stanley, *Make Your Garden New Again.* Simon & Schuster, 1975.

Staff of the L. H. Bailey Hortorium, Cornell University, *Hortus Third: A Dictionary of Plants Cultivated in the United States and Canada.* Macmillan Publishing Co., 1976.

Stoffel, Robert J., *Do's and Don'ts of Home Landscape Design.* Hearthside Press, 1968.

Sunset Editors, *Lawns and Ground Covers.* Lane Publishing Co., 1975.

Taylor, Norman, *Guide to Garden Trees and Shrubs.* Bonanza Books, 1965.

Taylor, Norman, ed., *Taylor's Encyclopedia of Gardening.* Houghton Mifflin Co., 1961.

Van Dersal, William R., *Why Does Your Garden Grow?* Quadrangle, 1977.

Voykin, Paul N., *A Perfect Lawn the Easy Way.* Rand McNally, 1969.

Voykin, Paul N., *Ask the Lawn Expert.* Macmillan Publishing Co., Inc., 1976.

Whitehead, Stanley B., *Garden Clematis.* John Gifford Ltd., 1959.

Wilson, Helen Van Pelt, *Successful Gardening in the Shade.* Doubleday & Co., Inc., 1975.

Wyman, Donald, *Ground Cover Plants.* The Macmillan Co., 1970.

Wyman, Donald, ed., *Shrubs and Vines for American Gardens.* Macmillan Publishing Co., Inc., 1969.

Wyman, Donald, *Wyman's Gardening Encyclopedia.* Macmillan Publishing Co., Inc., 1971.

Picture credits

The sources for the illustrations in this book are listed below. Credits from left to right are separated by semicolons, from top to bottom by dashes. Cover: Tom Tracy. 4: Frederick R. Allen. 6: Sonja Bullaty and Angelo Lomeo. 9-16: Drawings by Kathy Rebeiz. 19: Neil Kagan. 20, 21: Sonja Bullaty and Angelo Lomeo. 22, 23: John Neubauer. 24, 25: Tom Tracy. 26-29: Sonja Bullaty and Angelo Lomeo. 30, 31: John Neubauer. 32: Sonja Bullaty and Angelo Lomeo. 34, 36: Drawings by Kathy Rebeiz. 38: Constance Porter from Photo Researchers, Inc. 39: Russ Kinne from Photo Researchers, Inc. 41: John Neubauer. 42: Michael Alexander—Richard Jeffery. 43: Tom Tracy. 44: Drawing by Kathy Rebeiz. 46: Sonja Bullaty and Angelo Lomeo. 50-58: Drawings by Kathy Rebeiz. 61, 62: Sonja Bullaty and Angelo Lomeo. 63: Sonja Bullaty and Angelo Lomeo, except bottom, Richard Jeffery. 64, 65: Sonja Bullaty and Angelo Lomeo. 66, 67: John Neubauer. 68: Sonja Bullaty and Angelo Lomeo. 71: Drawing by Edward Frank. 75, 76: Drawings by Kathy Rebeiz. 79-81: John Neubauer. 82: Sonja Bullaty and Angelo Lomeo. 83: Bernard Askienazy, except top, John Neubauer. 84: Sonja Bullaty and Angelo Lomeo, except top left, John Neubauer. 85: Sonja Bullaty and Angelo Lomeo. 86: Illustration by Eduardo Salgado. 88–148: Illustrations by artists listed in alphabetical order: Richard Crist, Mary Kellner, Gwen Leighton, Allianora Rosse, Eduardo Salgado. 152, 153: Maps by Adolph E. Brotman.

Acknowledgments

The index for this book was prepared by Anita R. Beckerman. For their help in the preparation of this book, the editors wish to thank the following: Henry C. Allen, Cambridge, Mass.; B.C. Designs, Los Angeles, Calif.; Mrs. Ernesta D. Ballard and Frederic L. Ballard, Philadelphia, Pa.; Bishop White Garden, Independence National Historical Park, Philadelphia, Pa.; Dr. James W. Boodley, Professor of Floriculture, Cornell University, Ithaca, N.Y.; Sonja Bullaty and Angelo Lomeo, New York City; Mrs. Orville H. Bullett Jr., Berwyn, Pa.; Mr. and Mrs. Robert Coe, Alexandria, Va.; Joseph Copp, Los Angeles, Calif.; Mr. and Mrs. Earl Dibble, Scarsdale, N.Y.; Dough Dorough, landscape designer, Dorough Landscape Co., Atlanta, Ga.; Dr. Donald Egolf, Research Horticulturist, National Arboretum, Washington, D.C.; Entheos, Bainbridge Island, Wash.; Marnie Flook, Greenville, Del.; Galper Baldon Associates, Landscape Architecture & Land Planning, Venice, Calif.; Mr. and Mrs. Milton Goetz, Pelham, N.Y.; Harold Greer, Greer Gardens, Eugene, Ore.; Karl Grieshaber, New York Botanical Garden, Bronx, N.Y.; Mr. and Mrs. Jack Helfend, Los Angeles, Calif.; Victorine and Samuel Homsey, Architects, Wilmington, Del.; Dr. and Mrs. John E. Hopkins, Wayne, Pa.; Mrs. Louellyn Hutchinson, Seattle, Wash.; Mrs. George Isdale, Rye, N.Y.; Joann Knapp, Planting Fields Arboretum, Oyster Bay, N.Y.; Dr. and Mrs. John K. Knoor III, Gladwyne, Pa.; Alfred O. Krautter, Sprain Brook Nurseries, Scarsdale, N.Y.; Mareen Kruckeberg, Seattle, Wash.; Mr. and Mrs. Harold D. McCoy, Alexandria, Va.; Fred McGourty, Brooklyn Botanic Garden, Brooklyn, N.Y.; Macaire Gardens, Los Angeles, Calif.; Mr. and Mrs. Pendleton Miller, Seattle, Wash.; Erik Neumann, Curator of Education, National Arboretum, Washington, D.C.; Marvin Olinsky, New York Botanical Garden, Bronx, N.Y.; John P. Osborne, Westport, Conn.; Mrs. Emily Seaber Parcher, Sharon, Mass.; Frederick W. G. Peck, Chestnut Hill, Pa.; J. Liddon Pennock Jr., Meadowbrook Farm Greenhouse, Meadowbrook, Pa.; Sally Reath, Devon, Pa.; Pearl April Richlin, Sherman Oaks, Calif.; Mrs. Florence Robinson, Pelham, N.Y.; Louis Smirnow, Brookville, N.Y.; Kim Steele, Seattle, Wash.; Robert G. Titus, Planting Fields Arboretum, Oyster Bay, N.Y.; Mr. and Mrs. Corydon Wagner, Tacoma, Wash.; Mr. and Mrs. Walter F. Winkler, Brunswick, Me.; Nona Wolfran, Pan American Seed Company, West Chicago, Ill.; Mary Zalon, New Rochelle, N.Y.

Index

Numerals in italics indicate an illustration of the subject mentioned.